Introduction to Health & Social Care and Children & Young People's Settings

SECOND EDITION

Corinne Barker and Emma Ward

HODDER
EDUCATION
AN HACHETTE UK COMPANY

Orders: please contact Hachette UK Distribution, Hely Hutchinson Centre, Milton Road, Didcot, Oxfordshire, OX11 7HH. Telephone: +44 (0)1235 827827. Email education@hachette.co.uk Lines are open from 9 a.m. to 5 p.m., Monday to Friday. You can also order through our website: www.hoddereducation.co.uk

ISBN: 978 1 3983 2736 8

© Corinne Barker and Emma Ward 2021

First published in 2021 by
Hodder Education,
An Hachette UK Company
Carmelite House
50 Victoria Embankment
London EC4Y 0DZ

www.hoddereducation.co.uk

Impression number   10 9 8 7 6 5

Year   2025 2024

Cover photo © kmiragaya - stock.adobe.com

Illustrations by Integra Software Services Ltd.

Typeset in India by Integra Software Services Ltd.

Printed and bound by CPI Group (UK) Ltd, Croydon, CR0 4YY

A catalogue record for this title is available from the British Library.

Contents

Acknowledgements

We would like to thank colleagues and students at Wakefield College who have contributed ideas and taken such an interest in the writing of this textbook.
We would also like to thank the editorial team at Hodder Education, in particular, Ruth Murphy, publisher; Sylvia Bukowski, desk editor; and Kate Short, freelance copy-editor, for their support.
Corinne and Emma

Picture credits

The publishers would like to thank all the staff, children and families at Vanessa Nursery School, Ark Alpha Nursery, Godington Day Nursery and Kate Greenaway Nursery School and Children's Centre for their help with many of the photographs, taken by Jules Selmes, Andrew Callaghan, and Justin O'Hanlon. A special thanks to Michele Barrett and Julie Breading for all their assistance with the organisation of the photo-shoots.

Every effort has been made to trace the copyright holders of material reproduced here. The authors and publishers would like to thank the following for permission to reproduce copyright illustrations:

p.viii © Monkey Business – stock.adobe.com; p.2 © Tyler Olson – stock.adobe.com; p.4 © dglimages – stock.adobe.com; p.5 © Andrey Popov – stock.adobe.com; p.6 © Miguel Tamayo – stock.adobe.com; p.9 l © Viacheslav Iakobchuk – stock.adobe.com, r © Monkey Business – Fotolia.com; p.10 © Rawpixel.com – stock.adobe.com; p.12 © Andrew Callaghan – Hodder Education; p.13 © andreaobzerova – stock.adobe.com; p.19 t © drubig-photo – stock.adobe. com, b © Andrey Popov – stock.adobe.com; p.20 © Sandor Kacso – stock.adobe.com; p.21 © contrastwerkstatt – Fotolia.com; p.25 © WavebreakMediaMicro – stock.adobe.com; p.26 t © Deksbakh – stock.adobe.com, bl © WavebreakMediaMicro – stock.adobe.com, br © migstock – Alamy Stock Photo; p.27 © De Visu – stock.adobe.com; p.29 tl © Courtesy of Childline, a service provided by NSPCC, tr © Courtesy of NSPCC, bl © Refuge.org (www.refuge.org.uk), br Women's Aid (www.womensaid.org.uk); p.30 © fizkes – stock.adobe.com; p.31 © Alina555 – Getty Images; p.32 © Rido – stock.adobe.com; p.36 tl © LIGHTFIELD STUDIOS – stock.adobe.com, tr © Syda Productions – stock.adobe.com, m © Jules Selmes – Hodder Education, b © Dragana Gordic – stock.adobe.com; p.39 t © imageBROKER – Alamy Stock Photo, b © Magdalena Juillard – stock.adobe.com; p.40 t © Rawpixel.com – stock.adobe.com, b © Monkey Business – Fotolia. com; p.41 tl © Monkey Business – stock.adobe.com, br © contrastwerkstatt – stock.adobe. com, bl © pressmaster – stock.adobe.com, tr © Tetra Images, LLC – Alamy Stock Photo; p.42 t © Jules Selmes – Hodder Education, bl © Comeback Images – stock.adobe.com, br © Monkey Business – stock.adobe.com; p.44 t © Coolpicture – stock.adobe.com, b © Jules Selmes – Hodder Education; p.45 l © carballo – stock.adobe.com, r © IMAGEMORE Co., Ltd. – Alamy Stock Photo; p.48 © Rawpixel.com – stock.adobe.com; p.50 © Daisy Daisy – stock.adobe.com; p.51 t © nimito – stock.adobe.com, b © WavebreakmediaMicro – stock.adobe.com; p.54 © Africa Studio – stock.adobe.com; p.56 © mottto – stock.adobe.com; p.59 © Mark Richardson – Alamy Stock Photo; p.60 t © Satjawat – stock.adobe.com, bl © stocksolutions – Fotolia.com, br © Monika

How to use this book

Make real progress with this Introduction to Health & Social Care and Children & Young People's Settings! This book guides you through the 7 mandatory units and 15 optional units exploring safeguarding and communication to healthy eating, and growth and development. Each unit includes headings clearly matched to the specification and links to assessment criteria, as well as an array of activities to help you generate evidence.

What you will learn in this unit
Appearing at the beginning of each chapter, this box tells you what you will learn in the chapter.

Important words
These boxes explain the meaning of the words you will need to know for the qualification.

Example!
These boxes will give you examples of what is being discussed on the page.

Task
These boxes suggest things you can do to help you to understand the subjects that have been explained on the page. For example, you may be asked to discuss the subjects in pairs or as part of a group.

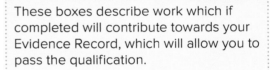
Assessment task
These boxes describe work which if completed will contribute towards your Evidence Record, which will allow you to pass the qualification.

Case study
An example of a real person or situation that helps illustrate the point in the chapter.

Summary
This box appears at the end of each chapter, and reminds you of what you should have learnt from reading the chapter.

Information
These boxes provide useful information and will help you remember key points.

Safety warning
These boxes highlight any important points regarding health and safety.

Part 1
Mandatory units

Chapter 1

INTRO MU 1.1 Understand the range of service provision and roles within health and social care (adults and children and young people), early years and childcare

What you will learn in this unit

You will gain an understanding of:

- the range of service provision available in health care and social care and childcare
- the difference between statutory and independent service provision
- how informal care contributes to service provision
- the different job roles within health care, social care and childcare, and the knowledge and skills required to carry out these roles
- progression routes for employment in health care, social care and childcare.

LO1 The range of service provision in health and social care, early years and childcare

1.1 **1.2** **1.3** **The range of service provision, the purpose of service provision and examples of who would access different types of service provision**

Types and purpose of service provision

There are many different types of health care, social care and childcare available for **service users** to use. Care services can be statutory, independent or informal and can include the following types of **service provision**, as listed in Table 1.1 on pages 2-4.

Important words

Service user – someone who uses the health, social or childcare services

Service provision – services that are available for people needing health care, social care or childcare

Type of service provision 1.1	Purpose of the provision 1.2	Who may access the service provision 1.3
Day care for adults	◆ Many care homes for adults with a disability have closed down, which means adults may want to continue to live in their own home ◆ Provides social activities for adults with a disability	Adults with a disability who need day-to-day support
Hospital accident and emergency department	◆ Provides emergency treatment when a person suddenly becomes seriously ill ◆ If someone has a dangerous or life-threatening accident	Everyone
Residential services for children and young people (foster care)	◆ Provides safe care for children and young people who cannot live with their own family	Children and young people
Tele care, e.g. 999 emergency service, Childline, Samaritans	◆ Provides medical advice to people who phone asking for help ◆ Supports people in times of crisis	Everyone in need of advice and support People who do not know where to go to get help

Table 1.1 Types and purpose of service provision, and who may use the provision

Figure 1.1 Telephone helplines

Type of service provision 1.1	Purpose of the provision 1.2	Who may access the service provision 1.3
Community-based services, e.g. home help, community nurses, meals service	◆ Provides care for people who need support to live in their own home ◆ Provides medical care for people who are ill but not staying in hospital ◆ Helps to provide for care needs (dressing, bathing, providing meals)	Older aged adults Anyone with a disability or additional need
Day nurseries	◆ Provides care and education for young children aged 0–5 years ◆ Needed by working families during working hours ◆ Allows children to socialise with others	Children and their families
Doctors' surgery (GP)	◆ Diagnoses and treats illness and gives prescriptions for medication ◆ Gives health care advice ◆ Organises support groups	Everyone
Complementary therapies	◆ Can be used instead of or alongside medical treatment, e.g. homeopathy, reflexology, massage	Everyone
Mental health services	◆ Diagnoses mental health conditions and provides a range of short- and long-term support	Everyone

Table 1.1 Types and purpose of service provision, and who may use the provision *(continued)*

Figure 1.2 Home help

Type of service provision 1.1	Purpose of the provision 1.2	Who may access the service provision 1.3
Community pharmacy (chemist)	◆ Gives out prescription medicine ◆ Sells non-prescription medicine and first aid supplies ◆ Offers health care support and advice, e.g. stopping smoking, contraception advice	Everyone
Substance misuse services	◆ Supports the safety of drug users (needle exchange) ◆ Offers counselling and rehabilitation services	People with addictions
Residential care home	◆ Provides full-time care for older aged adults who are no longer able to care for themselves ◆ Older aged adults can receive short-term care, e.g. to give their main carer a break	Older aged adults

Table 1.1 Types and purpose of service provision, and who may use the provision *(continued)*

Task

What services might these people use?

◆ A rugby player with a sporting injury
◆ A child with a chesty cough
◆ An older aged adult living in their own home who finds it difficult to cook their own meals
◆ A young person with an addiction

Assessment task 1.1 1.2 1.3

Identify at least two different providers of health, social or childcare services in your local area. For each one, explain the purpose of the provision and give an example of who would access the service. You can use a table like the one below:

Type of service	Purpose of service	Example of user of service

Table 1.2 Types and purpose of service provision in my local area, and who may use the provision

1.4 The difference between statutory and independent service provision

Figure 1.3 A carer in a private home

A *statutory service* should be available to everyone by law.

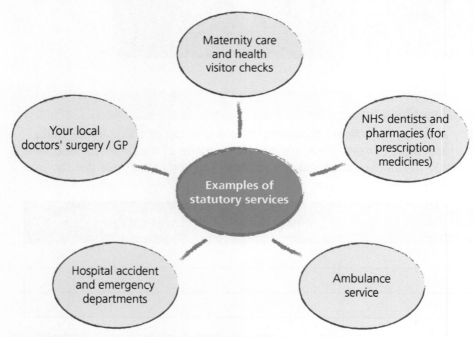

Figure 1.4 Examples of statutory services

An *independent service* does not have to be provided by law but can be provided by people or companies who charge for the service.

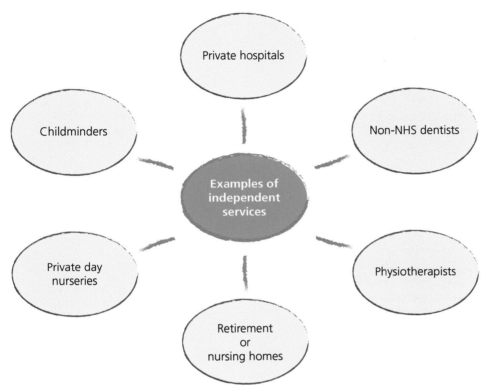

Figure 1.5 Examples of independent services

A *voluntary service* is provided by people who do not get paid and do not expect payment from the people who need help.

1.5 How informal care contributes to provision

Informal care may be given by family, friends, neighbours or members of the local community. This type of care may be provided for a short time; for example, if someone is recovering from an illness and cannot yet meet their own care needs (washing, cooking and cleaning), a neighbour may offer to help until they are able to do these things for themselves.

Informal care may also be long term – for example, a family member looking after an older aged parent so that they do not have to go into a care home. Informal care is very important within communities as it means that people do not always have to use statutory services, such as hospitals, which can sometimes become too full. It also means that anyone who cannot afford to pay for independent services can still be cared for.

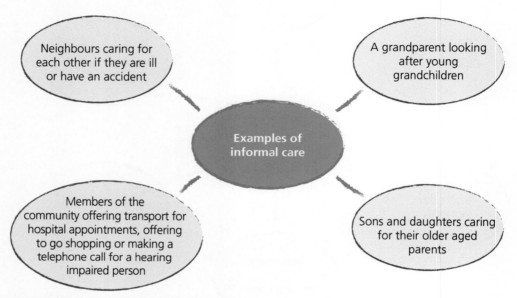

Figure 1.6 Examples of informal care

Task

Are the following services statutory or independent?
◆ A neighbour goes shopping for an older aged person.
◆ You have an appointment with your local doctor.
◆ A young person with anxiety sees a counsellor.
◆ An alcohol-dependent adult phones a helpline for help.

Assessment task 1.4 1.5

Make an information poster for service users to be displayed in a doctors' surgery that gives information about statutory services and independent services, and the differences between these services.

On your poster, give information about informal care and say how this can help different people who need support.

LO2 The range and scope of roles within health and social care, early years and childcare

2.1 Job roles within health care, social care and childcare

There are many **job roles** within health and social care and childcare. Some of these job roles are needed in all of these services – for example, receptionist, cleaner or health visitor. Other job roles are only needed in one of these types of service – for example, a midwife or doctor would only work within health care services.

Figure 1.7 A doctor examining a patient

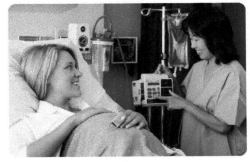

Figure 1.8 A midwife caring for a patient

Important words

Job role – the job that somebody working in the care sector does

Research – finding information, for example, from the internet, from books or by speaking to others

Assessment task 2.1

Research or discuss the list of job roles below and sort them into the correct service. Remember – some job roles may fit into more than one service.

- Health care assistant
- Health visitor
- Midwife
- Physiotherapist
- Play therapist
- Occupational therapist
- Receptionist
- Social worker
- Community care worker
- Cleaning staff
- Childcare worker
- Paramedic

Health care	Social care	Childcare

Table 1.3 Job roles within health care, social care and childcare

Figure 1.9 A paramedic attending an emergency callout

2.2 Knowledge and skills required to work in health and social care, early years and childcare

Every job role has its own set of roles and responsibilities. People need to have the correct **qualifications and skills** to be able to do certain jobs. For example:

◆ A *nurse* needs to have a nursing qualification before they are allowed to care for people. However, to do the job well they also need to be kind and caring, want to help others and have good communication skills.

◆ A *health care assistant* will sometimes have a qualification or experience in caring for people. They need to be reliable, patient, kind and caring, and be able to follow instructions and work as part of a team.

◆ A *nursery worker* in a day nursery will need to have a childcare qualification, but they will also need to follow all the policies and **procedures** carefully, be very reliable, and show patience and understanding towards the children.

◆ A *doctor* spends many years at university learning how to diagnose and treat illness. A doctor will need to be very interested in the health of others and be able to take responsibility for their care and treatment. Doctors need to be able to read and understand information so that they are aware of all the new treatments that become available.

Care home assistant wanted
at Sunnyvale Care Home

Level 2 in Health and Social Care preferred

Experience of working in a care home is not necessary as training will be given. We are looking for the right person to join our team of carers. Your key qualities:

- you are able to work well in a team
- you follow procedures
- you are kind, patient and caring towards others

Figure 1.10 Example of a job advertisement

Important words

Qualifications and skills – the training or courses you need to complete and the things you need to be good at to do the job well

Procedures – steps to take when doing a task

Assessment task 2.2

Choose two job roles from the list on page 9. Research the knowledge and skills required to work in these jobs.

(It may help you if you look on the internet and read job descriptions for particular job roles.)

2.3 Progression routes for a worker within the sector

Once a health, social or childcare worker has qualified to do a job, they may decide that they would like to progress within the service and take **employment** in a different role with more responsibility or challenges. This is called **progression**.

Important words

Employment – a job that you are paid to do

Progression (in a career) – being able to move on to the job you want to do, or to get a promotion

Example!

Josh, a nursery worker, looks at what the nursery manager does every day and decides that in the future, when he has more experience, that will be the job role he would like to do. It is important that Josh finds out about any further qualifications he needs or skills he will need to develop, in order to reach his goal of becoming a nursery manager.

Ruby has worked as a ward cleaner on a children's ward in a hospital for ten years. She watches the hospital play therapist who works with sick children and decides this would be her dream job. Her children have now all left home and she feels it is the right time to further her

career and train as a play therapist. Ruby did not get many qualifications at school so she is going to college in the evening to get the qualifications she needs to apply for this training.

Assessment task 2.3

Iram works in a children's centre and enjoys her job, but she has always been interested in becoming a midwife.

Describe the progression route that Iram must take to become a midwife. (It may help you to research midwifery courses available at university and the qualifications needed to apply.)

Summary

In this unit, you have learned that:

- there are a range of services provided for health and social care, early years and childcare
- the services provide for the different needs of different people
- there is a difference between statutory and independent service provision
- informal care has an important role in contributing to service provision
- there are many different job roles in health and social care, early years and childcare, and there are many different skills required to carry out these roles
- a progression route is the journey taken to get the qualifications and skills needed to do a particular job role.

Chapter 2

INTRO MU 1.2 Understand the principles and values in health and social care (adults and children and young people), early years and childcare

What you will learn in this unit

You will gain an understanding of:

◆ the principles and values that support work in health and social care, early years and childcare
◆ the guidance and standards that support work in health and social care, early years and childcare
◆ respecting and valuing service users as individuals
◆ person-centred and child-centred practice
◆ how confidentiality helps show respect for individuals.

LO1 The principles and values that underpin work in health and social care, early years and childcare

1.1 The principles and values that support work in health and social care, early years and childcare

We all have different **principles and values** that we learn from the people around us. This might be school rules we have to follow or the way we are expected to behave at home. For example, one family may expect shoes to be taken off at the front door, but another family may not think that this is important and wear shoes or boots around the house. Both of these families have principles and values that are different, but are right for them.

Important words

Principles and values – the main beliefs and ideas of an organisation

When working in health, social care and childcare, it is important to know that we must follow the values and principles of the setting rather than our own because sometimes a practitioner's own values may stop them from working in a professional way.

There are many important principles and values that health, social care and childcare workers need to understand so that they always work in a professional way. This is important to make sure that all children and adults using services are respected and well cared for.

Figure 2.1 Examples of values and principles that support work in health and social care and childcare

1.2 Guidance and standards that support the principles and values

Guidance and standards are the rules that should be understood to make sure that the values and principles are followed correctly by everyone working in the setting.

> ### Important words
>
> **Guidance and standards** – rules and guidelines that should be followed

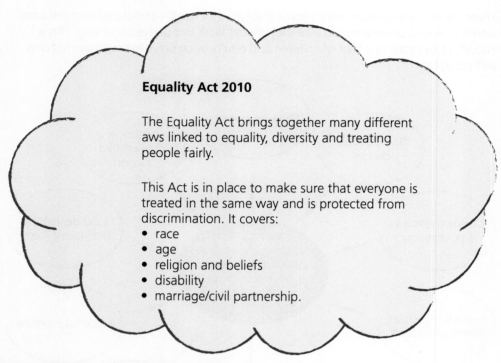

Equality Act 2010

The Equality Act brings together many different aws linked to equality, diversity and treating people fairly.

This Act is in place to make sure that everyone is treated in the same way and is protected from discrimination. It covers:
- race
- age
- religion and beliefs
- disability
- marriage/civil partnership.

Figure 2.2 Equality Act 2010 guidelines

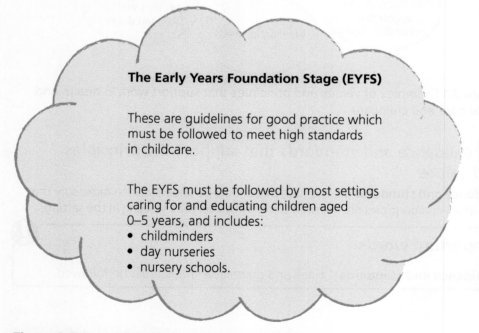

The Early Years Foundation Stage (EYFS)

These are guidelines for good practice which must be followed to meet high standards in childcare.

The EYFS must be followed by most settings caring for and educating children aged 0–5 years, and includes:
- childminders
- day nurseries
- nursery schools.

Figure 2.3 Early Years Foundation Stage guidelines

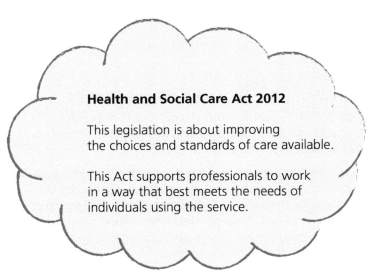

Health and Social Care Act 2012

This legislation is about improving the choices and standards of care available.

This Act supports professionals to work in a way that best meets the needs of individuals using the service.

Figure 2.4 Health and Social Care Act standards

Assessment task 1.1 1.2 2.1

Make a leaflet that could be given to a new practitioner working in a health centre to tell them about:

◆ the guidance and standards that give us understanding of values and principles in health and social care and childcare
◆ the values and principles that support work in health and social care and childcare
◆ the need to value and respect service users as individuals.

LO2 Ways to respect and value individuals who access services in health and social care, early years and childcare

2.1 Respecting and valuing service users as individuals

The guidance and standards looked at in this chapter are in place to make sure everyone working in health, social care and childcare works in a way that respects and values the needs and wishes of everyone.

It is important that people who use services are respected and valued as individuals so that they *feel valued as people*. By listening to the wishes, needs, likes and dislikes of individuals, and showing you value someone's opinion, that person may *feel more confident in making choices for themselves*. By **respecting and valuing** service users, a *more trusting relationship will develop* between them and care workers and this will help the service user to feel more *in control of their own lives*.

When people know that others are interested in their views and opinions, it helps to make them feel respected and valued.

Important words

Respecting and valuing – to show care and consideration of others' views and opinions

2.2 2.3 Ways to value children, young people and adults

Ways to value children and young people	Ways to value adults
Observe them to find out their likes and dislikes.	Give them time to speak and listen carefully.
Provide activities that they are interested in.	Communicate with them in a way that suits their needs.
Ask for their opinion and give them choices.	Ask about their needs and wishes.
Respect cultural and family values.	Allow them to make decisions about their daily care **routines**.

Table 2.1 Ways to value children, young people and adults

Important word

Routines – tasks or activities which happen regularly during the day, usually at a set time; for example, mealtimes and bedtimes

Assessment task 2.2 2.3

In pairs, discuss and write down one more way to value:

◆ children in a primary school   ◆ young people who use care services.

Figure 2.5 Children at primary school

Task

Jack is 82 years old and has moved into a care home. Dani, a care worker, helps Jack with some of his daily care routines and plans activities that she thinks Jack will enjoy. Give examples of ways Dani can value Jack and show him respect.

2.4 Person-centred and child-centred practice

Person-centred practice is listening to a person's needs, wishes, likes and dislikes and understanding the importance of meeting their individual needs, in a way that is right for them.

By using person-centred practice, the needs and choices of an individual person are seen as very important.

A service that offers the same care to everyone and does not offer different care to meet individual needs is *not* providing *person-centred practice.*

An example of person-centred practice is a doctor in a hospital asking an older aged adult if they want their medicine as a liquid or a tablet, as both are suitable. By allowing the adult to make choices about their care, the doctor is valuing their opinion and respecting their wishes.

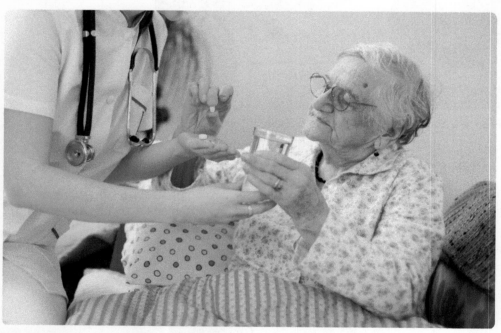

Figure 2.6 Person-centred practice

Child-centred practice is understanding what individual children need and giving them the right care and support.

A setting that offers the same activities or routines to all children and does not offer different support to meet individual needs is *not* providing *child-centred practice.*

An example of child-centred practice is when a practitioner working in a day nursery allows children to choose which food they would like to eat, rather than giving all children the same snack.

Important words

Person-centred practice – listening to a person and meeting their individual needs in the way that is best for them

Child-centred practice – meeting children's individual needs and understanding their interests so they can enjoy taking part in activities

2.5 Confidentiality

Confidentiality means keeping an individual's private information safe and only sharing this information with people who need to know – for example, sharing information with other practitioners who are involved in supporting the health and care of children and adults.

There is a law that everyone in Europe must follow, including everyone working in health and social care and childcare. This law is called the General Data Protection Regulation (GDPR) and it tells everyone exactly how to store, record and share information correctly.

Confidentiality is kept when people working in health, social care and childcare follow GDPR and know how to keep information private. All personal information must be stored safely – for example, on a password-protected computer or in a locked cupboard. When you are working in health, social care or childcare you may need to know about a person's family background, health or financial situation, so it is important that you can always be trusted with personal information.

Figure 2.7 Doctors only share private information with people who need to know

Important word

Confidentiality – only sharing information with people who need to know or can offer help

2.6 How confidentiality helps show respect for individuals

Confidentiality helps to show respect and values individuals for many reasons; for example, it supports an individual's **self-esteem** because they will feel confident if they know that their private information will only be shared with other professionals who are caring for them.

If an individual thought that their private information was not safe and could be shared with people who may not protect them, it would make them feel very worried and would affect their confidence and self-esteem.

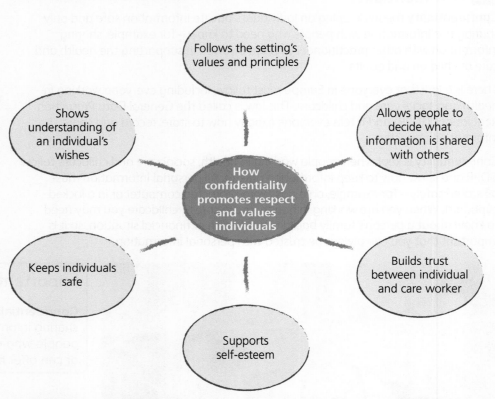

Figure 2.8 How confidentiality promotes respect and values individuals

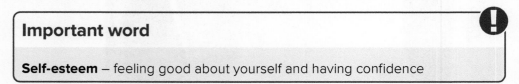

Important word

Self-esteem – feeling good about yourself and having confidence

Summary

In this unit, you have learned that:

◆ there are principles and values that support work in health and social care, early years and childcare
◆ the guidance and standards that support work in health and social care, early years and childcare must be followed
◆ respecting and valuing service users as individuals is very important
◆ person-centred and child-centred practice is about putting the individual's needs first
◆ there is a law called GDPR that everyone working in health, social care and childcare in Europe must follow to protect an individual's personal information
◆ confidentiality must be kept to make sure individuals are respected and valued.

Chapter 3

What you will learn in this unit

You will gain an understanding of:

- keeping children, young people and adults safe from harm, abuse and neglect
- signs of harm, abuse and neglect to look out for
- what to do if you are worried that someone is being harmed, abused or neglected
- support available to keep people safe
- places that offer information about keeping people safe.

LO1 Protection in health and social care, early years and childcare

1.1 Protection of vulnerable adults

Protecting **vulnerable adults** means **preventing abuse** from taking place or acting quickly when you suspect abuse may be taking place.

Protecting vulnerable adults is very important when working in health and social care. This is because many people who need health and social care services could be easily hurt or feel hurt by the way they are treated. People using health and social care services often rely on health workers to give them the support and care they need to be happy and healthy.

Important words

Vulnerable adult – someone who could be abused easily or hurt through neglect or unkindness

Preventing – trying to stop something from happening

Abuse – to be treated in a damaging way by one or more people

Figure 3.1 Supporting vulnerable people to be happy

1.2 Child protection

Children need to be protected from **harm**, abuse and **neglect** as they are vulnerable. This is because they are young and are not always able to make choices or decisions for themselves. Protecting children from all types of harm, abuse and neglect is known as **safeguarding**. Responsible and caring adults can help to make sure that the **environment** and the people in that environment keep children safe.

> ### Important words
>
> **Harm** – injury or hurt caused to someone
>
> **Neglect** – when someone is not looked after or cared for properly
>
> **Safeguarding** – protecting children and adults from harm, abuse or neglect
>
> **Environment** – the space around the child

Figure 3.2 Child playing in a safe environment

Figure 3.3 Children need to be protected from harm, abuse and neglect

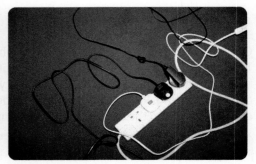

Figure 3.4 Power cords should be kept out of reach of children

1.2 **1.3** Protecting children and vulnerable adults from harm, abuse and neglect

Harm is when someone gets hurt because of neglect or abuse.

Abuse is when a person or people treat someone very badly.
- An example of *physical abuse* is when an adult hurts a child on purpose or an older aged adult in a care home is handled roughly.
- Abuse can also be *emotional abuse*; an example of this is when a person keeps saying hurtful words that make someone feel upset or bad about themselves.
- *Sexual abuse* is when children, young people or vulnerable adults are used for sexual acts or are forced to be involved in making or seeing sexual images.

Neglect is when a person's needs are not met; these may be emotional needs or physical care needs.

- Children who are neglected will often have health problems, such as illness which is not treated, or development problems, such as not becoming fully toilet trained at the expected age.
- Adults who are neglected may also become ill due to not being given healthy food or not having enough warmth.
- Older aged adults may feel neglected or lonely if no one comes to visit them and ignores their needs, such as not getting the help they need to eat, drink, take their medicines or keep themselves clean.

Figure 3.5 Vulnerable adults need to be protected

Assessment task 1.1 1.2 1.3

Produce an information leaflet for health and social care students going into placement for the first time. You need to describe each of the following:
- protection of vulnerable adults
- safeguarding children.

Add information to this leaflet to explain what is meant by 'harm, abuse and neglect' when protecting vulnerable adults.

1.4 Examples of indicators of abuse and neglect

Physical abuse	Emotional abuse	Sexual abuse	Neglect
◆ Broken bones ◆ Burns, bruises or bites that are not explained ◆ Fear ◆ Depression ◆ Untreated injuries ◆ Not wanting to change for PE or swimming lessons	◆ Depression ◆ Mood changes ◆ Aggressive behaviour ◆ Child becomes clingy ◆ Attention-seeking ◆ Low self-esteem ◆ Sleep or speech problems ◆ Running away ◆ Drug or alcohol misuse	◆ A child has too much knowledge about sex ◆ Urine infections ◆ Eating problems (anorexia or bulimia) ◆ Sleep problems or nightmares ◆ Bed wetting ◆ Pregnancy ◆ Sexually transmitted diseases	◆ Hunger/thirst ◆ Poor diet (given only junk food) ◆ Untreated illness ◆ Not being given prescribed medicines ◆ Bed sores ◆ Unwashed clothes ◆ Missing school ◆ Being left alone ◆ Being harmed through unsafe environment

Table 3.1 Examples of indicators of abuse and neglect

Assessment task 1.4

On the leaflet for health and social care students, write down three signs of:
◆ physical abuse
◆ emotional abuse
◆ sexual abuse
◆ neglect.

Task

Jamila is being cared for in a residential home. The carers have the job of making sure that the residents are safe and well cared for. Sadly, Jamila trips over a wire that is trailing from a heater and burns her leg. Discuss whether you feel this is neglect or an accident.

Ethan, aged two, goes to a local nursery two days each week. His mum collects him in the afternoon and finds that his nappy has not been changed all day. The nappy is heavy and wet, and Ethan has a sore nappy rash. Discuss whether you feel this is abuse, neglect or neither.

1.5 Actions to take when there are concerns about harm, abuse or neglect

When someone is worried that a child or adult is at risk of harm, abuse or neglect, there are important steps to take to help that person. It is important to act confidentially: that means that the concerns are not talked about to anyone apart from the setting supervisor, police or professionals from **support organisations**.

Figure 3.6 Many organisations offer online advice and telephone helplines

When there is a concern about a person being harmed, abused or neglected, the first step is to write down the facts. If the concern is in the workplace – for example, in a children's nursery, a hospital or a residential home – the first action would be to talk to the supervisor or the person responsible for safeguarding, clearly explaining what the concerns are. The person responsible for dealing with reports of abuse or neglect will investigate the concern and tell the police, social services or other organisations, if necessary.

Important words

Support organisations – organisations such as Childline, the NSPCC and Women's Aid which work to protect children and adults

---

If the concern relates to something outside of work, it is still important to report it or signpost the person to the following organisations for help and support. The police force has officers who are experienced in dealing with protection and safeguarding of adults and children. There are many organisations such as Childline, National Society for the Prevention of Cruelty to Children (NSPCC), Refuge and Women's Aid which offer online advice and telephone helplines to use when there are concerns about a person's safety. Again, it is important that the concerns are not discussed with anyone other than the people who can help, as confidentiality must be kept.

Figure 3.7 Telephone helplines

Assessment task 1.5

On the leaflet for health and social care students, write down what the students should do if they are worried about someone being harmed, abused or neglected.

1.6 Confidentiality and when to share information

Confidentiality means only sharing information with people who need to know or can offer help and support. The person responsible for protection and safeguarding in the workplace will have a very good understanding of confidentiality and will know what to do to keep information private. If someone is at risk of serious harm or abuse, the information will be shared quickly with the police or other organisations that can help to keep the person safe or get them to a safe place quickly. All personal information must be stored safely – for example, on a password-protected computer or in a locked cupboard.

Assessment task 1.6

On the leaflet for health and social care students, write down:
◆ why it is important to understand confidentiality
◆ when it is important to share information.

1.7 Responsibility for safeguarding

Information should only be shared with people who need to know the facts or who can offer protection, such as the police, child protection officers, social services, safeguarding professionals or setting managers. Sometimes the setting managers, social services or the police will decide to share the information with parents or main carers if they think it is necessary.

Figure 3.8 Share information only if it is necessary

Task

In pairs or small groups, read the information above and make a list of people or organisations responsible for protecting vulnerable adults and safeguarding children.

Assessment task 1.7

On the leaflet you are making, include some information about the people who have responsibility for safeguarding.

1.8 The role of organisations in safeguarding

Organisations such as schools, nurseries, care homes and day care centres for older aged adults and adults with disabilities all have a responsibility to protect children and adults. To protect everyone, organisations should have written policies that describe how to protect and safeguard everyone working in or using the service. Each setting will have written guidance that clearly explains what should be done when there is a concern about harm, abuse or neglect.

Everyone who works in any of these organisations or settings will have safeguarding training so they know what to do if they have a concern. This guidance or training will also include steps to take if someone is worried that a care worker is not treating people properly – for example, shouting unkindly at a child or not taking care of a vulnerable adult.

Task

A care worker goes into the home of an older aged man most days to help him to get showered and dressed. The care worker is worried when the man tells her that he is glad that she has come today because the other care worker shouts at him for being too slow and that she sometimes hurts him when she helps him dress.

What should the care worker do now that she knows this might be happening?

Assessment task 1.8

On your leaflet for health and social care students, write down what organisations can do to protect children and vulnerable adults.

1.9 Support available for people experiencing harm, abuse or neglect

Support is also available for people who deal with cases of harm, abuse or neglect as they too may be affected in some way; for example, they may feel upset or concerned that they should have been able to do more to help.

Examples of sources of support are provided in the box below.

Information

The Samaritans
The Samaritans is a charity available 24 hours a day offering confidential advice and support to anyone in distress. They also work to raise awareness of issues such as suicide and depression.
www.samaritans.org

Seeking counselling?
Your GP
Remember that your own GP or health centre is a good place to find out what NHS-funded services you may be able to access with a GP referral.

Worried about a young person being bullied or abused?
Kidscape
Kidscape is committed to keeping children safe from abuse. Kidscape is the first charity in the UK established specifically to prevent bullying and child sexual abuse. The helpline is for the use of parents, guardians or concerned relatives and friends of bullied children. If you are a child and are experiencing bullying problems, you should visit or ring Childline.
www.kidscape.org.uk

Worried about a young person?
Childline
Whatever your worry, it's better out than in. Call Childline for help.
www.childline.org.uk

NSPCC
The aim of the NSPCC is to protect children from cruelty, support vulnerable families, campaign for changes to the law and raise awareness about abuse.
www.nspcc.org.uk

Worried about a vulnerable adult?
National Crime Agency
A national support agency that provides help, advice and guidance to vulnerable individuals and victims of crime.
https://nationalcrimeagency.gov.uk

Source: Information from www.excellencegateway.org.uk

Task

Can you find out about other sources of support or information about protection and safeguarding?

You could look for leaflets in doctors' surgeries, Citizens Advice centres or chemists, or search for information on the internet.

Assessment task 1.9

At the end of your leaflet, list some sources of support linked to protection and safeguarding.

Summary

In this unit, you have learned that:

- it is important to keep children, young people and vulnerable adults safe from harm, abuse and neglect
- there are many ways that harm, abuse and neglect can take place and there are many signs that show this may be happening
- it is important to take the right actions if you are worried that someone is being harmed, abused or neglected
- confidentiality is very important and information must be shared and stored safely
- there are many professions and organisations that offer support and help to keep people safe.

Chapter 4

INTRO MU 1.6 Introduction to communication in health and social care (adults and children and young people), early years and childcare

What you will learn in this unit

You will gain an understanding of:

- different ways to communicate with children and adults
- barriers that stop communication happening
- methods that may help to break down communication barriers.

What is communication? Communication is a way of getting or giving information.

Good communication is very important when you are working with others or looking after people. You often need to get information from people, such as what they need or how they feel. You might need to give information to others – for example, telling them the time of their appointment or where the carer will meet them.

LO1 Different methods of communication

1.1 Communication methods

People communicate with each other in lots of different ways and for lots of different reasons. These **communication methods** may include:

- **Verbal communication** – this is when information is given thorough speaking and listening.
- **Non-verbal communication** – this is when information is given through body language, hand gestures and facial expressions.

Important words

Communication methods – ways to communicate

Verbal communication – speaking and listening

Non-verbal communication – ways to communicate without speaking

Figure 4.1 The nurse is asking this person how he feels

Figure 4.2 The health care worker is reading a text message

Task

Can you decide what the childcare worker and the health care worker in these photos are trying to say through their body language and hand gestures?

Sometimes other types of non-verbal communication are needed; for example, a hearing-impaired person may use sign language such as Makaton to communicate.

Written communication – this is when information is written down in a letter, email or text; for example, a shopping list, an appointment reminder or a bus timetable.

Pictures and visual communication – this is when pictures and signs are used to help an individual understand information; for example, a hand-washing poster will help a young child who cannot read to understand how to wash their hands properly.

Figure 4.3 An appointment reminder by text

Figure 4.4 Written communication and pictures

Task

Can you think of any other examples of communication using pictures or signs?

Assessment task 1.1

Make a spider diagram identifying at least five different communication methods.

Skills needed to communicate

Lots of skills are needed to communicate well. These include the skills listed below.

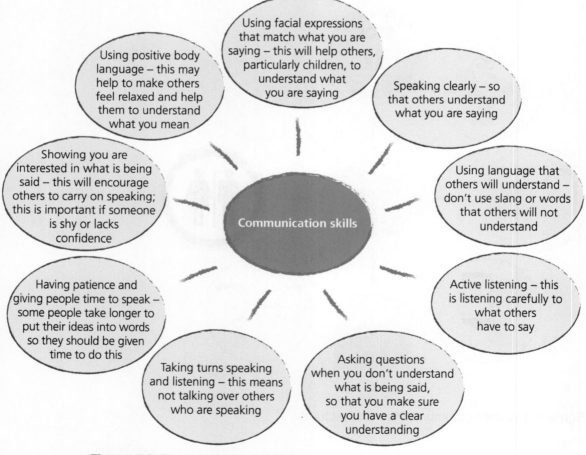

Figure 4.5 Communication skills

Types of communication include:

◆ *One to one*: This means two people are having a conversation. To do this well, each person will be talking clearly, listening carefully, using facial expressions (for example, smiling) and using body language (for example, nodding their head, or using hand movements).

◆ *Group discussions*: This is when communication is taking place with more than one person – for example, a teacher explaining the rules of a game to a group of children, or a team of carers discussing how to improve the activities provided for the older aged residents in a care home.

Figure 4.6 The teacher is using clear language that the children can understand

Figure 4.7 The practitioner and the older aged person are engaging in a game of draughts

Informal communication

Informal communication usually takes place between people who know each other well or between family members – for example, friends chatting in the school playground or a family talking during meal times.

Figure 4.8 Friends chatting in the school playground

Figure 4.9 A family talking during meal time

> ### Important words
>
> **Informal communication** – speaking with friends

Formal communication

Formal communication often happens in the workplace, for example, a midwife in a health centre discussing care needs with a pregnant woman. Another example of formal communication is when a group of early years workers meet the nursery manager to plan play activities for children.

During formal communication it is important to speak clearly and use appropriate language. This is because communication is an important part of being a care professional.

> ### Important words
>
> **Formal communication** – when information is shared in a professional way; slang words are not used

Figure 4.10 The midwife needs to give the pregnant woman information about a healthy diet

Figure 4.11 A doctor comforting a patient

Figure 4.12 A business meeting over coffee

Figure 4.13 The nurse manager asks the team to share their ideas

Figure 4.14 A childminder and a child, playing

When people communicate in groups, it is important that everyone is given the chance to speak and be listened to. This is a good way for lots of ideas or feelings to be shared, especially when important decisions need to be made. Often someone may be very good at speaking but not good at listening to what is being said. This is a **barrier** to communication because everyone's views and opinions will not be heard.

> ## Important word
>
> **Barrier** – something that gets in a person's way and may stop them from doing something

Figure 4.15 Social workers discussing the needs of families

Figure 4.16 A carer supporting an activity

2.1 Finding out about the communication needs of individuals

Communication is very important in health and social care and early years care. By taking time to find out how best to communicate with someone, or finding ways to help a person communicate and be understood, you may make life a lot happier for someone who usually finds communication difficult.

It is very important to find out the communication and language needs of others. This could include understanding ways to improve communication with a person.

Ways to improve communication	Example
Ask questions	What time would you like your lunch?
Observe the individual	Watch the child communicate with friends to see how their language skills are developing
Ask other people who may have useful information	Ask parents or family members how best to communicate with a person close to them
Talk to the carers of individuals	
Read case notes or personal records	

Table 4.1 Understanding ways to improve communication with a person

Just asking questions about how best to communicate with someone will help to support good communication. Sometimes others such as parents, family or support services can help you to understand how best to communicate with someone. Health care workers will often look at a person's records or care plan to see if there is any information about how best to communicate with that person.

Identifying individual communication needs

When working with people of all ages, from babies to older aged adults or people with disabilities, it is really important to communicate in an appropriate way so that good communication takes place. It is important to use good communication skills so that the correct information is given and easily understood. Some people have different communication needs and it is the job of a health care or early years worker to find out these needs and look for ways to communicate well.

Parents and carers use a type of communication with babies called 'parentese'. This involves speaking in a higher than usual pitch, sometimes in a sing-song voice, often repeating words or simple sentences.

Figure 4.17 Parents use a type of communication with babies called 'parentese'

The parents or carer will give lots of eye contact and use lots of positive facial expressions, such as smiling. Babies communicate through different sounding cries, and as they begin to gurgle and babble, this is the beginning of communication skills.

Figure 4.18 Eye contact and smiling are important

Figure 4.19 Young people often use mobile phones to text or talk

Figure 4.20 Hearing impairments can make communication difficult

Some young people prefer to communicate with their friends through the use of mobile phones or computers to text, talk, email or access social media websites.

Communication impairments

When a person has a hearing impairment, they may find communication difficult. Often a person will use some type of hearing aid to help them hear more easily. Sign language such as Makaton can be used to help children with communication difficulties.

Some children's TV programmes support children with communication needs by using Makaton. See **www.bbc.co.uk/cbeebies/shows/something-special/**

Assessment task 2.1

Robin is 14 years old. He has a hearing and speech impairment, and finds communicating difficult. Robin cannot always easily communicate his needs, wishes and preferences.

In pairs, discuss and write down how practitioners can understand how Robin prefers to communicate his needs, wishes and preferences to others.

2.2 2.3 Barriers to communication and overcoming barriers to communication

A barrier to communication is anything that stops good communication taking place.

This could be a *language barrier*, where perhaps two people speak different languages; an *environmental barrier*, such as a very noisy room; or an *emotional barrier*, when perhaps someone is too upset to give or receive communication.

Another barrier could be a **physical barrier**, when perhaps someone is visually impaired and cannot see the facial expressions or body language, which would make it difficult to understand if someone was being serious or not. A *hearing barrier* is when a person is not able to hear clearly, or perhaps has no hearing at all.

A *cultural barrier* is when an acceptable way to communicate in some cultures, such as pointing to a sign, is seen as rude by other cultures. In most cultures, it is important to give good eye contact when speaking; however, in a few cultures, giving eye contact to other people when speaking is seen as very rude.

Social barriers could include using words that others do not understand or speaking in a way that makes others feel uncomfortable.

It is important to find ways to overcome barriers to communication so that a person's needs, wishes and preferences can be understood.

Important words

Physical barrier – when someone is stopped from taking part in an activity because the environment and/or equipment does not meet their individual needs

Social barrier – the way people are treated by others which can stop them being included or taking part in an activity

Assessment task 2.2 2.3

Complete the table on page 47 to show barriers to communication and ways to overcome these barriers.

Barriers to communication	Ways to overcome the barriers to communication
Children, older adults or wheelchair users who may be lower down than others	Make sure you get down to the same level as others so that you can make good eye contact and allow the child or adult to feel included
	Use an interpreter to communicate information
Loud, noisy room where it is difficult to clearly hear what others are saying	
Cultural differences in using hand signs or eye contact	Be aware that some cultures have different meanings for some hand signs and that eye contact can be seen as threatening or disrespectful within some cultures
Not showing respect	Make sure you ask a person the name they prefer you to use when speaking to them, e.g. 'Mrs Green' rather than saying 'Sunita' or 'love'
When people use slang words or complicated words	
	Make sure that if the person uses a hearing aid, it is switched on
	Use sign language or other communication methods that the person prefers
Lack of confidence in communicating with other people – for example, speaking in a group or talking to a doctor or social worker	Using positive facial expressions, such as smiling, and positive body language, such as nodding, may help a person feel more relaxed

Table 4.2 Barriers to communication and how they can be overcome

Summary

In this unit, you have learned that:

- there are many different ways to communicate with children and adults
- people may have individual communication and language needs and preferences that should be recognised
- there are a range of barriers that make it difficult for communication to be clearly understood
- barriers to communication can be overcome when appropriate ways to communicate are found.

Chapter 5

PWCS 03 Introductory awareness of equality and inclusion in health, social care and children's and young people's settings

What you will learn in this unit

You will gain an understanding of:

◆ the importance of equality and inclusion within health, social care and children's and young people's settings
◆ the effects of discriminatory attitudes and behaviours on individuals
◆ social and physical barriers that may prevent equality and inclusion
◆ ways to overcome barriers that prevent equality and inclusion
◆ the behaviours that may promote equality and inclusion.

LO1 The importance of equality and inclusion within health, social care and children's and young people's settings

1.1 1.2 Equality and inclusion and how they form the basis for the principles and values of health, social care and children's and young people's settings

Inclusion is making sure everyone can be included

Equality is about making sure all people are treated fairly

Figure 5.1 Equality and inclusion

All organisations have principles and values, which everyone should be aware of, to help them to work in a way that is both fair and meets the needs of everyone using the service.

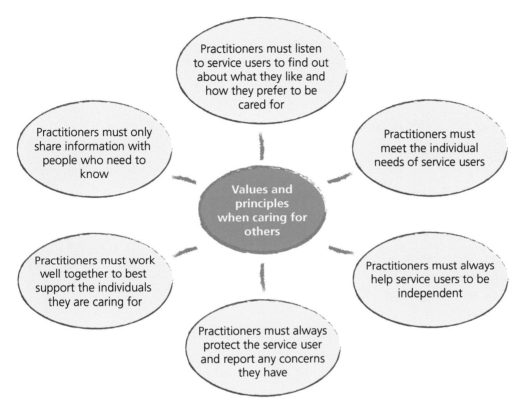

Figure 5.2 Values and principles when caring for others

Equality and **inclusion** are both important to the principles and values of a setting. There is **legislation** (laws) that must be followed to support equality and inclusion. This important legislation includes:

◆ Equality Act 2010
◆ Early Years Foundation Stage (EYFS)
◆ General Data Protection Regulations (GDPR)
◆ Health and Social Care Act 2012.

Important words

Equality – making sure all people are treated fairly

Inclusion – being part of something, and making sure everyone is included in a fair and equal way

Legislation – laws or rules which must be followed

Assessment task 1.1 1.2

Make a colourful wall poster which:

◆ shows the meaning of the terms 'equality' and 'inclusion'
◆ names the legislation (laws) that supports equality and inclusion
◆ shows values and principles practitioners must follow when working in care services.

LO2 The effects of discriminatory attitudes and behaviours on individuals

2.1 Discriminatory attitudes

Discrimination is the treatment of an individual based on the group or category to which the person belongs. For example:

◆ age
◆ gender
◆ language
◆ cultural background
◆ religion
◆ choice of partner (LGBTQ)
◆ disability.

Figure 5.3 A young person in a wheelchair being included in a basketball game

A **discriminatory attitude** is when someone judges another person or group of people because of the way they look, how they speak, their age, the clothes they choose to wear or who they choose to have a relationship with.

Figure 5.4 Being discriminated against may make people feel very unhappy

2.2 How discriminatory attitudes can affect individuals

When a person is discriminated against, they may feel left out of the group or they may feel no one understands them. This may make them feel very unhappy or very bad about themselves.

Figure 5.5 Left out of the group

Important word

Discriminatory attitude – when someone judges another person or group of people because of the way they look, how they speak, their age, the clothes they choose to wear or who they choose to have a relationship with, for example

Being discriminated against can make a person feel worthless and they may choose not to get involved in activities in the setting or mix with others in the group. This could affect their care or education because they may not feel they want to attend the setting. They may become isolated and want to stay in their own home; they may feel afraid for their safety, or even become ill or have poor mental health. This could then stop them being able to work or form healthy relationships with others.

Assessment task 2.1 2.2

Think about what you now know about discriminatory attitudes and complete the table below by identifying how discriminatory attitudes can affect individuals.

Identify discriminatory attitudes towards ...	Give examples of discriminatory attitudes towards these individuals	How discriminatory attitudes can affect these individuals
a person aged 65 years	May not be interviewed for a job when there are younger applicants	◆ May not feel valued ◆ May become depressed ◆ May struggle to pay their bills
a young person in a wheelchair		
same-sex couples		

Table 5.1 How discriminatory attitudes can affect individuals

2.3 Discriminatory behaviours

Discriminatory behaviour is the unfair way one person may treat another because of the differences between them. For example, young people in a secondary school may leave another young person out of the group because they dress differently or prefer different music.

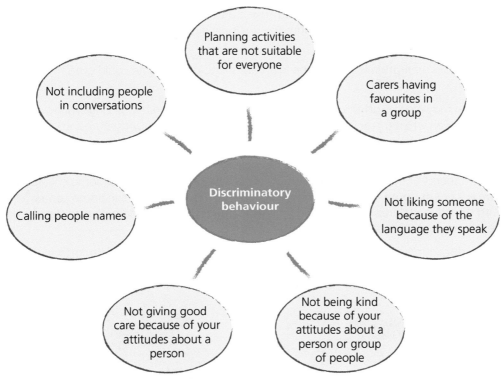

Figure 5.6 Discriminatory behaviours

Important word

Discriminatory behaviour – when someone treats another person or group of people differently because of the way they look, how they speak, the music they listen to or the clothes they choose to wear, for example

2.4 How discriminatory behaviours can affect individuals

Discriminatory behaviours may result in someone not having the care and help that they need and deserve. The person may feel very unhappy or their needs may not be met; they may be neglected or even worse become ill.

For example, if a carer does not give the time and care to a person because of the differences between them, they may not notice a health problem. This is very poor practice and the carer could damage the individual's health or they could lose their job.

Because discrimination is against the law, carers who discriminate could even be taken to court.

Children may also be affected by discriminatory behaviours in the setting. This may happen when a practitioner has an opinion about the family background of the child or discriminates against children from a different culture.

Discrimination can sometimes happen by accident – for example, the pretend food practitioners put in the home corner may not be the kind of foods that some children's families eat at home. This might mean that the child does not use the home corner with the other children in the setting. This may affect the child's learning and social development as they are not joining in.

When discrimination happens, a child may become upset and not want to attend the setting so they may miss out on learning new things.

Figure 5.7 Different people come from different family backgrounds

Using what you have learned about discriminatory behaviours, complete the table below to identify how discriminatory behaviours can affect individuals.

Identify discriminatory behaviours	Give examples of how discriminatory behaviours can affect individuals
Not including all older aged residents with hearing impairments in a game of bingo	
An older aged same-sex couple who cannot live independently any more not being offered sheltered accommodation	The couple may not get the care and support they need. They may not feel valued and could have health problems due to not being given the care they need.
Practitioners in a primary school not providing children with books that show people from different cultures and backgrounds	

Table 5.2 How discriminatory behaviours can affect individuals

3.1 Social and physical barriers that may prevent equality and inclusion

Social barriers that may prevent equality and inclusion in settings can be something as simple as not being made to feel welcome within a group. Social barriers can also include not having the confidence to join in with activities or talk to others in the group.

If a carer or other person in the group has acted in a discriminatory way towards an individual, the individual may feel afraid to join in, or may want to stay out of the way in case something happens to upset them.

Another social barrier might be a learning difficulty, which means that a person is not able to communicate or socialise with others confidently. People with a sight or hearing impairment may not have an equal chance to take part in all activities if their needs are not met when activities or routines are provided.

Physical barriers may include having a physical disability which is not thought about by carers when they are planning activities for the whole group. Other physical barriers include not having the special equipment needed or enough space to move around safely.

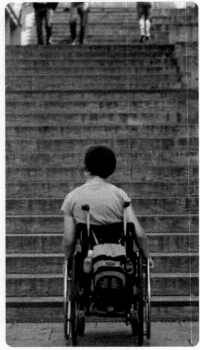

Figure 5.8 Physical barriers

3.2 How barriers to equality and inclusion may be overcome

All barriers to equality and inclusion can be overcome by using a person-centred approach when planning activities and providing care. It is important that carers think about the individual needs and skills of every person in the group and find ways to make sure they are all included.

Carers may need to find out about any special equipment that might help a person to feel included. Equality and inclusion training is important for carers to understand how they can find out about the needs of children and young people, and meet those needs.

3.3 Behaviours that may promote equality and inclusion

Carers as professionals must be good role models and always include everyone in activities and routines. When carers behave in a positive way and treat everyone fairly, others will see that this is the right way to treat people and will copy this behaviour. Carers must act quickly to stop any discriminatory behaviour.

If carers do not step in when they see discriminatory behaviour, others in the group may think it is acceptable to behave this way and people could carry on being hurt.

Assessment task 3.1 3.2 3.3

Create a leaflet which gives information about equality and inclusion. The leaflet should include:

◆ a list of social and physical barriers that may prevent equality and inclusion
◆ ways these barriers can be removed
◆ an example of positive behaviour that supports equality and inclusion.

Summary

In this unit, you have learned that:

◆ it is important to maintain equality and inclusion in health, social care and children's and young people's settings
◆ discriminatory attitudes and behaviour can hurt individuals
◆ social and physical barriers may stop equality and inclusion
◆ there are many ways to remove the barriers which prevent equality and inclusion
◆ people's behaviour can promote equality and inclusion.

Chapter 6

PWCS 04 Introductory awareness of health and safety in health, social care and children's and young people's settings

What you will learn in this unit

You will gain an understanding of:

◆ the key areas of health and safety related to work settings
◆ employers' and workers' responsibilities for health and safety
◆ health and safety training required in the work setting
◆ risk assessments in relation to health and safety
◆ the importance of protecting the safety and security of all individuals in the work setting
◆ accidents and illness that may take place in work settings and who might deal with them
◆ how infection is spread in the workplace
◆ ways to reduce the spread of infection in health, social care and children's and young people's settings.

LO1 The main responsibilities of workers and employers for health and safety in health, social care and children's and young people's settings

1.1 1.2 1.3 Key areas and responsibilities for health and safety related to the work setting

When working in health, social care and children's and young people's settings, it is very important to work in a way that keeps everyone safe and healthy. Organisations (**employers**) need to have written procedures which contain rules about how to work safely, and these must be checked regularly to make sure that they will support a safe working environment. Organisations must provide equipment and training needed to keep everyone safe.

Workers (**employees**) must always follow all of the setting procedures so that they work in a way that keeps themselves and others safe. They must always use the protective equipment available in the work setting.

> ## Important words
>
> **Employer** – someone or an organisation that pays workers for their work
>
> **Employee** – a worker

There are seven key areas of health and safety that we need to know about:
1 Fire safety
2 Moving and handling
3 First aid
4 Security
5 Storage and disposal of hazardous substances
6 Medication storage and administration
7 Infection prevention and control

Fire safety

All organisations need to have a plan in case of fire. This plan will include how to get out of a building quickly and safely. There has to be a clearly signed exit route out of the building. It is law that these exits are kept clear and the doors can be opened easily in the event of a fire.

It is also part of the law that firefighting equipment, such as fire extinguishers and fire blankets, are kept in good working order. Most settings will have fire alarm systems that must be tested regularly so that in the event of a fire, a loud alarm will warn people to **evacuate** the building quickly.

Settings will have regular fire evacuation practices so that in the event of a real fire, everyone would know how to get out of the building quickly and safely. All fire evacuations, whether real or just practices, must be recorded.

Figure 6.1 A fire blanket

> ## Important word
>
> **Evacuate** – leave a building or area safely

Moving and handling

When working with children, people with illness or physical disability or older aged adults, a care worker may need to help them to move around. It is important that this is done in a way that does not cause any injury or pain to the person being moved or to the care worker. Therefore, organisations must make sure that workers know how to move people around safely.

Special equipment and training on how to use this equipment and how to move people safely must be provided by organisations so that care workers know how to move people around safely.

Figure 6.2 A care worker helping an older person

First aid

Accidents do happen, so it is very important that if a child or an adult has an accident, they can be helped quickly and safely. Every organisation must make sure that some or all of the care workers have a first aid qualification so if an accident happens, the person who is hurt can quickly receive the right care and treatment.

First aiders must make sure that they work in a way that keeps them and the injured person safe. This means wearing protective clothing and gloves if they are dealing with blood.

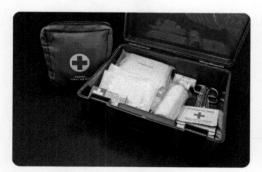

Figure 6.3 A first aid box

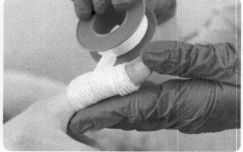

Figure 6.4 Protective gloves

First aiders will know when it is right to treat a person themselves because the injury is not serious, but they will also understand when the injury *is* serious and it is necessary to get medical help quickly.

The first aider must record all accidents that happen in an accident book, which must be signed by the first aider and the person who is injured. If a child is injured, then the parents must be informed and asked to sign the accident book.

> ## Important words
>
> **First aider** – someone with a first aid qualification

Security

All organisations must know who is in the building at all times; this includes care workers, people using the services and visitors. When they arrive at the work setting, care workers usually have to sign in using a register, code or swipe card.

Organisations are required to make sure that everyone is safe, so doors to a setting, such as a care home or nursery, will be locked so that children and vulnerable adults are not able to walk out on their own. It is usual for organisations to have a visitors' book that must be signed when someone visits the setting.

Figure 6.5 Swipe entry system

Storage and disposal of hazardous substances

Care organisations or care workers often have to use or store hazardous substances and materials.

Hazardous substances can be cleaning products, chemicals or medicines used in the care and treatment of adults and children. Nappy waste, blood products and equipment such as used needles are also hazardous materials.

It is the law (Control of Substances Hazardous to Health, **COSHH**) that all organisations must store hazardous substances safely, use them in a safe way and then dispose of them safely (**safe disposal**). All chemicals must be stored in a locked cupboard that is only opened by people allowed to do so.

When chemicals are brought into a setting, there has to be a risk assessment. The assessment will give instructions on how to use the chemicals safely and what to do if the chemicals are spilled or used incorrectly.

Records must be kept to show that any hazardous waste has been disposed of safely – for example, by use of a special bin collection service.

Important words

COSHH – the law linking to the **C**ontrol **of S**ubstances that are **H**azardous to **H**ealth

Safe disposal – to throw away safely

Figure 6.6 Hazardous substances

Medication storage and administration

When organisations or care workers have to store and give medication to children and adults, there are very strict rules to follow. This is because if medicines are given to the wrong person, or the wrong amount is given to an adult or child, it could cause them serious harm or even death.

Organisations must provide locked storage cupboards and make a record of all medicines that are stored. When medicines are given to adults, this must be done by a qualified person, such as a nurse or care worker, and they must record the time and amount given.

When giving medicines prescribed by a doctor, nursery workers in a setting must have written permission from the parent or carer before they are able to give the medicine to the child. All medicines given to children must also be recorded, and the record signed by the nursery nurse and the parent.

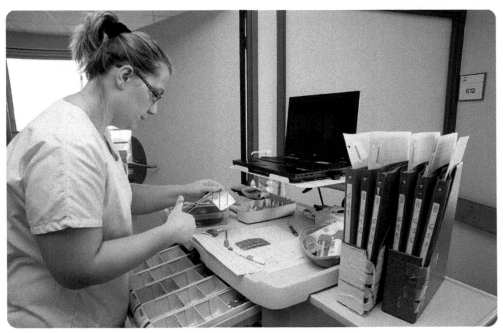

Figure 6.7 A nurse dispensing medicines

Infection prevention and control

All organisations must have policies and procedures which show that the prevention and control of infection has been thought about carefully. Procedures are steps which must be followed by everyone, such as:

◆ *Hand-washing procedures* – warm water and soap are always available and hand drying is carried out properly to try and reduce the spread of germs and infection.

◆ *Nappy changing procedures* – protective aprons and gloves are used and the area well cleaned after every nappy change to stop the spread of any infection. Nappies and cleaning cloths must be disposed of in a special bin.

◆ *Needle disposal procedures* – all used needles must be placed in a special bin where they cannot be removed. When full, the bin is taken away by a registered waste disposal company.

◆ *Body fluids procedures* – vomit, urine, faeces and blood are all body products which can contain germs and infection; therefore, they must be cleaned up and disposed of in a controlled way using protective clothing, separate cleaning equipment and special waste bins.

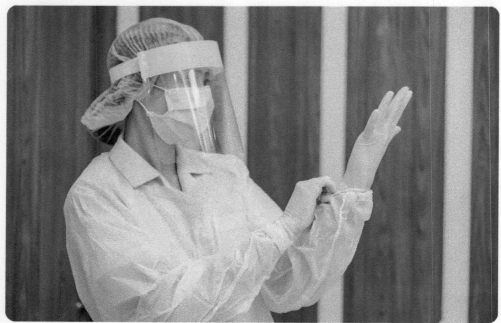

Figure 6.8 A carer wearing protective clothing

1.4 Health and safety training required in the work setting

All workers in health, social care and children's and young people's settings will need to have some health and safety training. This could include:

- training to learn about setting policies and procedures and how to follow them correctly
- first aid training
- safe moving and handling training
- COSHH (hazardous substance) training
- fire evacuation training.

Assessment task 1.1 1.2 1.3 1.4

You are room leader in a day nursery. You are asked to make an information leaflet for a new childcare worker, explaining:

- the key areas of health and safety they need to know about
- their responsibilities as a worker, for health and safety
- the manager's responsibilities for health and safety
- the health and safety training they will need to do
- when they must use personal protective equipment (PPE).

LO2 The importance of assessing risk in relation to health and safety

2.1 2.2 Hazards and risks

A hazard is something that can cause injury or harm to a person or group of people. A risk is what can happen as the result of a hazard. For example:

Hazard	Risk
A tray with cups left on the stairs in a care home	People tripping over the tray and falling on the stairs
The soiled nappy bin	If left open, young children might put their hands into the bin and develop an infection
The chemical storage cupboard	
Bags left in front of an emergency exit	
Spilled water on a care home floor	
Trailing wires and cables	

Table 6.1 Examples of hazards and risks

Assessment task 2.1 2.2

Write down what is meant by risk.

Complete the table above to show examples of risks.

2.3 Risk assessments

A risk assessment is completed to show where the dangers are in a work setting (the hazard).

The risk assessment will also show what might happen (the risk) if the hazard is not identified.

The risk assessment should show ways to try and get rid of the hazard, or reduce the risk of injury or harm (the control).

The hazard	The risk	The control
Objects left on the stairs in a care home	People tripping over the objects and falling on the stairs	Make sure items are never placed on the stairs
Hot drinks	Burns or scalds to children and adults	◆ Never carry hot drinks around a work setting ◆ Always place hot drinks on a work surface in the staff area ◆ Hot drinks should be at a safe temperature before being served to others

Table 6.2 Example of a risk assessment

2.4 Know when a risk assessment needs to be carried out

A risk assessment should be carried out and checked regularly to make sure that a work setting is safe for everyone. A risk assessment should also be carried out when:

◆ a child or adult has different needs (such as a wheelchair user)
◆ new equipment is brought into the work setting
◆ new staff join the setting
◆ an accident happens in the work setting
◆ it has been six months since the last risk assessment was carried out.

Assessment task 2.3 2.4

Make a health and safety poster which tells new staff about the importance of risk assessments and when a risk assessment should be carried out.

LO3 The importance of key areas of health and safety in relation to health, social care and children's and young people's settings

3.1 The importance of protecting your own security and the security of others in the work setting

It is the law that all workers protect themselves and others in the work setting. This can be done by always following work setting procedures.

By following procedures, tasks are always carried out in the safest way. Workers who do their job properly, by always following procedures correctly, keep themselves safe and secure. This is because if there is an accident or something goes wrong in the setting, and all procedures have been followed, they will not be to blame.

If workers do not follow procedures correctly and something goes wrong, they are breaking the law and may lose their job.

3.2 The importance of safe moving and handling

When working in health, social care and children's and young people's settings, people and equipment must be moved safely, so that no one is injured.

- Care workers may need to help older aged adults to get out of bed, or help them into the bath, so it is important that they have training to do this safely.
- Nursery workers will need to safely lift babies and young children in and out of highchairs and cots.

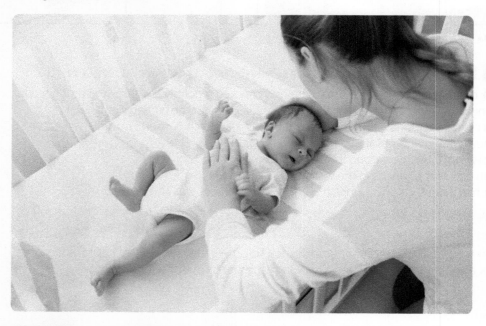

Figure 6.9 Nursery workers need proper training to safely handle children

Work settings will provide the training but it is the responsibility of the care worker to always carry out moving and handling in the correct way. This is important because if they try to save time or do not use equipment properly, they could cause harm or injury to themselves or the people they are caring for.

3.3 3.4 Accidents and illness that may occur in work settings and who might deal with them

When an accident happens in a setting, it must always be reported to the first aider, who will deal with the injured child or adult. If everyone in the setting is first aid trained, the first aider who is nearest to the accident would deal with it.

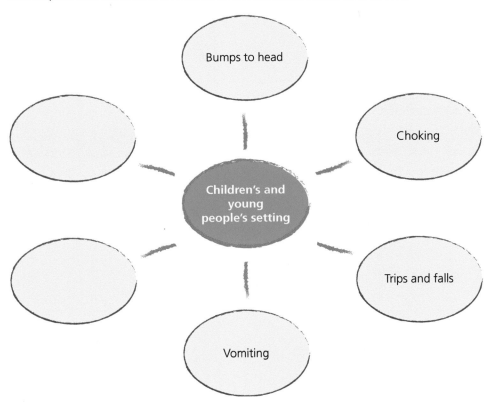

Figure 6.10 Accidents and sudden illness that could occur in children's and young people's settings

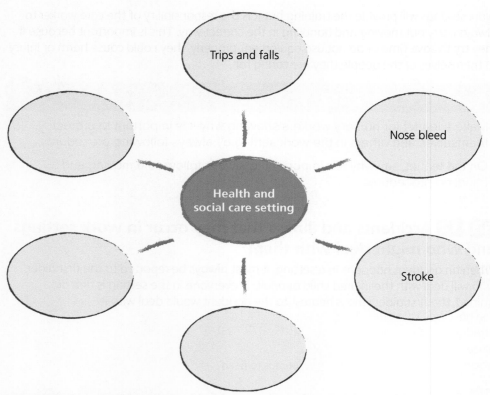

Trips and falls

Nose bleed

Health and
social care setting

Stroke

Figure 6.11 Accidents and sudden illness that could occur in health and
social care settings

Assessment task 3.3 3.4

Complete the spider diagrams to show accidents and sudden illness that may
occur in both of the settings.

Say who might deal with the accidents and illness.

LO4 Reducing the spread of infection in health, social care and children's and young people's settings

4.1 How infection is spread in the workplace

Infection can be spread in many ways. A few of these ways include:

◆ not following hand-washing procedures
◆ not following disposal of body fluid procedures
◆ sharing towels
◆ not wearing personal protective equipment
◆ sharing feeding equipment
◆ not cleaning toys properly
◆ attending the setting when unwell or with an infection
◆ unclean surfaces.

4.2 Ways to reduce the spread of infection in health, social care and children's and young people's settings

The best way to reduce the spread of infection is to make sure that there is a high standard of cleanliness and everyone in the setting follows all of the health and safety procedures. Young children and some adults will need to be supported to carry out procedures properly, such as hand-washing, toileting or wearing PPE.

4.3 The standard method of washing hands

Correct hand-washing is the best way to prevent the spread of infection in a setting. So it is very important that everyone washes and dries their hands properly.

There are five steps that need to be followed in hand-washing correctly:

1 Wet your hands using clean, warm water.
2 Using soap, lather your hands by rubbing them together.
3 Clean between the fingers and under your nails, scrubbing to the count of 20.
4 Rinse hands well in clean, running water.
5 Dry hands well using an air dryer or separate hand towel.

Source: **www.uhb.nhs.uk/Downloads/pdf/HandHygienePoster.pdf**

Assessment task 4.1 4.2 4.3

Make an information poster to put up in a care home, showing:

◆ how infection can be spread
◆ ways to reduce the spread of infection
◆ the best way to wash hands properly.

4.4 When personal protective equipment should be used

Personal protective equipment is known as PPE.

Examples of personal protective equipment

Gloves, aprons, eye goggles, face visors and face masks are all examples of PPE that may be worn when working in health and social care.

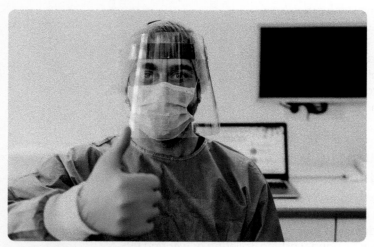

Figure 6.12 PPE equipment

PPE is used by practitioners caring for service users to avoid spreading infection or to stop them from coming into contact with body fluids such as blood, saliva or urine. PPE may sometimes be used by the service user's family – for example, if they are helping with washing or toileting.

- Getting germs onto your hands is one of the easiest ways of spreading infection, which is why hand-washing is so important.

- Wearing disposable gloves is another way to protect the practitioner and service user. Gloves protect hands from coming into direct contact with the germs and help to reduce the spread of germs to others.

- Face masks help to stop small droplets of saliva that leave our mouths when we speak or cough, infecting others. Masks also protect us from breathing in germs that may be in the air around us.

- Disposable aprons worn by a practitioner when caring for a service user must be changed before caring for a different service user. Changing aprons between service users helps to stop the spread of infection because any blood, urine or other bodily fluid that can carry germs will be on the apron that is thrown away and not on the practitioner's clothing.

Using the internet, find out why practitioners may need to use eye protection when working in some health care jobs.

Summary

In this unit, you have learned that:

◆ there are key areas of health and safety related to work settings

◆ employers and workers have responsibilities for health and safety

◆ health and safety training is required in the work setting

◆ risk assessments are used in relation to health and safety

◆ it is important to protect the safety and security of all individuals in the work setting

◆ accidents and illness may take place in work settings and there are people who are trained to deal with them

◆ infection can spread in the workplace if procedures are not followed correctly

◆ there are ways to reduce the spread of infection in health, social care and children's and young people's settings.

Chapter 7

PWCS 05 Introductory awareness of person-centred support in health, social care and children's and young people's settings

What you will learn in this unit

You will gain an understanding of:
- ◆ what is meant by person-centred support
- ◆ the benefits of person-centred support
- ◆ how to provide person-centred support
- ◆ how individuals can be in control of their care needs
- ◆ how risk assessments can assist person-centred support.

LO1 What is meant by person-centred support in health, social care and children's and young people's settings

1.1 What is person-centred support?

Person-centred support is about putting the needs and wishes of a person first. This is done by listening to a person and understanding the importance of meeting their individual needs, in a way that is right for them.

This is very different from giving support which is not person-centred, where a service may be offered even if it does not meet all of the person's needs.

Figure 7.1 A care worker listening to an adult

1.2 The importance of finding out an individual's history, needs, wishes, likes and dislikes

It is very important to ask children and adults about their wishes, likes and dislikes so that you understand what care and support would be best for them. It is also very important to find out about a person's history (this could be their medical history or a **life event**) so that the person can be supported in a sensitive and effective way.

Sometimes people are not able to tell you what they want or need, so you will need to communicate with others who may have this information, such as family members, parents and nursery or care workers.

If time is not taken to get this important information about a person's history, needs, wishes, likes and dislikes, the wrong help might be offered or the person may not feel their needs are being met. This could make them feel unhappy, lonely, worried or even unwell.

Important words

Life event – something that has happened to a person that has affected their life, such as serious illness or loss of a family member

Assessment task 1.1 1.2

Using the scenario below, outline the importance of finding out about Ben's history, needs, wishes, likes and dislikes.

Ben is two years old and will be starting nursery soon. Ben's mum is a little worried about him starting nursery as up to now he has only been cared for by family members. She wants Ben to be happy and stay healthy when he is at nursery. Ben has had a few health problems and is allergic to all milk products. Ben is not really interested in listening to stories or playing with jigsaws, but loves to be outdoors climbing and riding on sit-on toys. Ben's mum has started potty training Ben, but he still has a few accidents during the day.

1.3 How to provide person-centred support when supporting individuals in day-to-day activities

By using *person-centred practice*, the needs and choices of an individual person are seen as very important.

- A care worker providing care for an older aged adult in the home should take the time to find out about their needs and wishes. This means that they can support the individual in their care routine in a way that best suits them.
- For example, helping the individual to shower in the morning rather than the evening as that is what they would prefer.

Child-centred practice is the same as person-centred practice. This is when the individual care and learning needs of a child are met in a way that is best for them.

- It is good practice to ask a child about their interests, likes and dislikes when planning activities so that their ideas can be included.
- For example, if a child is interested in dinosaurs, an activity could be planned to include dinosaurs. When caring for very young children, it is important to get information about the child's likes and dislikes from parents or carers.

Assessment task 1.3

Discuss person-centred practice in groups. Write down more examples of how to provide person-centred support when caring for older aged adults.

LO2 The importance to individuals of person-centred support in health, social care and children's and young people's settings

2.1 The benefits of person-centred support

When person-centred support is given, the individual will feel valued and respected because they will know that their opinions and wishes are being listened to. This will help them to feel in control of what is happening in their lives. They may feel more confident about making choices and may feel happier doing things for themselves.

An example of person-centred support

Derek, aged 72, has had a mild stroke and needs some help to get dressed. Norma, his carer, knows that if she gives Derek a little more time to get dressed, he can do most of it on his own. It would be quicker for Norma to dress Derek herself, but she understands that Derek wants to be as independent as possible and do things for himself if he can. With this person-centred support, Derek is able to complete tasks for himself so feels valued and confident.

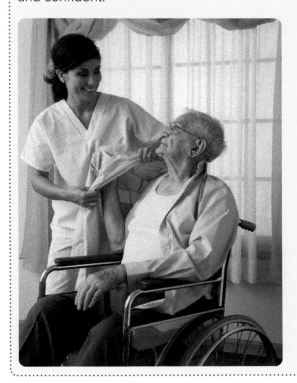

Assessment task 2.1 2.2

Discuss other benefits for Derek of being given person-centred support.

Fill in the gaps in the table on page 78 to show other ways that allow individuals to be in control of their care needs.

2.2 How individuals can be in control of their own care needs

It is important that individuals are supported to be in control of their own care needs. This is mostly done through individuals making their own decisions or being given suitable choices.

Look at the table below and decide how individuals can be supported to take control of their care needs.

Care need	Ways to support children and adults to be in control of their care needs
Maintain body temperature	Choice of wearing more clothing to keep warm or, where possible, turning up the heating Choice of removing a jumper or opening a window if they feel too warm
Sleep and rest	
Suitable clothes – dress and undress	
Personal hygiene	
Food and drink	
Fresh air and exercise	Children should be supervised so that they can choose to play indoors or outdoors Older aged adults can be given a choice of activities, such as swimming or walking in the garden

Table 7.1 Ways to support children and adults to be in control of their care needs

2.3 How assessing risk can assist person-centred support

If there are many risks in the environment, it is more likely that a person will come to harm. It is important to look at the environment and, where possible, reduce the chance of a child or adult being injured or harmed. This is done through **assessing risks** and putting **safety controls** in place to try to remove as many risks as possible.

> ### Important words
>
> **Assessing risk** – seeing something that might be a danger to someone
>
> **Safety control** – things that can be done to reduce the risk of injury
>
> **Assist** – help

For example, if the water temperature in a care home is controlled so that tap water is never too hot, then residents can take a bath when they want to, without needing to have a carer to check that the water is at the right temperature. This will give the resident more independence in their care routines and allows them to have some control to make choices.

By having low sinks and toilets in a day nursery, children who want to use the toilet independently can do so safely, without having to be taken by a childcare worker. This allows the child to be in control of their own care needs and supports their growing independence. This is an example of child-centred support.

Figure 7.2 Low sinks and toilets support a child's growing independence

Assessment task 2.3

Discuss another way that assessing risk might **assist** person-centred support.

Summary

In this unit, you have learned that:

- there are many benefits of person-centred support
- there are many ways to give person-centred support
- person-centred support helps individuals to be in control of their care needs
- risk assessments can assist person-centred support.

Part 2
Optional units

Chapter 8

PWCS 06 Introductory awareness of working with others in health, social care and children's and young people's settings

What you will learn in this unit

You will gain an understanding of:

◆ the importance of working with others in health, social care and children's and young people's settings
◆ ways of working with others
◆ ways of working with others that work well
◆ ways of working with others that do not work well
◆ the meaning and benefits of partnership working.

LO1 Know how to work together with others

1.1 The importance of working with others

In health, social care and children's and young people's settings, there are many different services offered, such as health care, childcare or homecare services. There are a wide range of people and professionals, with different skills, who work hard to provide these services. Each one of these people has an important job to do, but they could not do their job well without working with other people.

Figure 8.1 Some doctors work in a health centre with other health care professionals

There are many services offered in a health centre, for example. Doctors, health visitors, nurses, care workers, mental health nurses and **dieticians** all work together to keep everyone in the community as healthy as possible.

As well as health care professionals, there are other workers, such as cooks, receptionists, cleaners and office staff.

Important word

Dietician – a person who gives advice on healthy food and diet

Example!

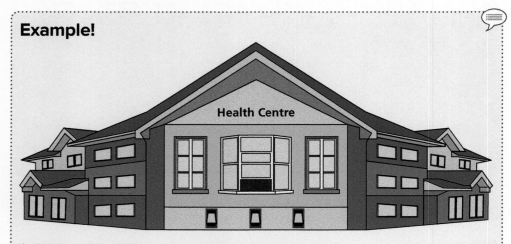

A doctor in a health centre has a room where people are seen and treated. People who need to see the doctor will first speak to a receptionist, who will book them an appointment. The health centre rooms need to be very clean, so cleaning staff have an important job to do.

It is important that all professionals and others with different jobs to do work together, so that they can provide the very best service.

1.2 Ways of working with others

There are many ways that professionals and others can work together to make sure that the people using the service are well cared for and the service is the best that it can be.

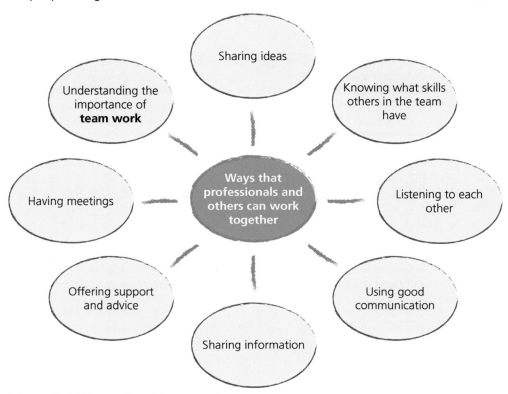

Figure 8.2 Ways of working together

Important words

Team work – when people work well together

Assessment task 1.1 1.2

Make a leaflet for health care workers about the importance of working with others:

◆ Say why it is important to work with others.
◆ Write down some ways to work with others.

1.3 1.4 Ways that work well and ways that do not work well when working with others

Some things that people do, and the ways that they do them, can mean the difference between working well together and not working well together.

There are examples of this in the table below:

Ways that work well when working with others	Ways that do not work well when working with others
Listening to what people say and trying to see their point of view	Listening to others' ideas but not taking any notice of their point of view
Going to meetings and sharing ideas	Going to meetings and not sharing your ideas
Getting to work on time and being reliable	Being late and not letting others know where you are
Understanding your own job role and making sure you work within it	Taking over tasks that other people are responsible for and that you are not trained to do
Speaking clearly and using appropriate language	Not speaking clearly and using slang
Offering support and help	Not helping when someone is struggling
Asking for advice when you need it	Doing everything your own way even if you could work better with help from others

Table 8.1 Ways of working with others

Assessment task 1.3 1.4

Add information to your leaflet about:
◆ ways that work well when working with others
◆ ways that do not work well when working with others.

LO2 Partnership working in health, social care and children's and young people's settings

2.1 2.2 The meaning of partnership working and examples of who partners may be

Partnership working is when people from different settings or with different skills come together to support individuals or share ideas to solve problems.

Partnership working can take place between workers in a setting or with other professionals who work outside of the setting. Sometimes different settings may work together in partnership to share equipment, staff and ideas.

> ## Important words
>
>
> **Partnership working** – when different professionals with different knowledge and skills work together to best support service users

> ## Example!
>
>
> A young child in a nursery with a speech and language difficulty may have the support of a speech therapist who comes into the nursery to support the child. The speech therapist will also share ideas with the nursery staff so they understand how best to support the child. The speech therapist and the nursery staff will meet regularly with the child's parents or carers to share information about the child's progress.

Examples of partners in health, social care and children's and young people's settings are:

- nursery workers
- the families of service users
- care workers
- doctors
- health visitors
- speech therapists
- occupational therapists
- receptionists
- cleaning staff
- school nurses
- teachers
- special educational needs co-ordinators.

Figure 8.3 Supporting a child

2.3 The benefits of partnership working

There are many benefits of partnership working in health, social care and children's and young people's settings, and these include:

- the correct support being available
- people being seen and treated sooner
- skills being shared
- information being shared appropriately
- equipment being shared
- staff sharing ideas
- professionals learning new skills from each other
- watching the way others work and learning from this.

Assessment task 2.1 2.2 2.3

Add information to your leaflet about:

- what partnership working means
- who practitioners may need to work in partnership with
- the benefits of partnership working.

Summary

In this unit, you have learned that:

- it is important to work with others in health, social care and children's and young people's settings
- there are many ways of working with others
- there are some ways of working with others that work well
- there are some ways of working with others that do not work well
- there are many benefits of partnership working in health, social care and children's and young people's settings.

Chapter 9

PWCS 07 Introductory awareness of the importance of healthy eating and drinking for adults

What you will learn in this unit

You will gain an understanding of:

- ◆ the importance of healthy eating
- ◆ what is meant by a balanced diet
- ◆ ways to inform people about the importance of a balanced diet
- ◆ the importance of drinking enough fluids to stay healthy
- ◆ signs that a person is not drinking enough fluids
- ◆ ways to encourage individuals to drink enough to stay healthy.

LO1 The importance of healthy eating

1.1 1.3 Balanced diets and the ways food can help people stay healthy

The main food groups

For children and young people to grow properly and be healthy, they need to eat a range of healthy foods that contain important **nutrients**. This is called a **balanced diet**. Adults should also eat a balanced diet to help them stay fit and healthy.

Important words

Nutrients – found in food; they do an important job to keep the body healthy

Balanced diet – daily food that has the right amount of nutrients for health and growth

To have a balanced diet, everybody should make sure that they eat foods from the five main food groups every day.

The five main food groups are:
- carbohydrates – wholegrain bread, cereals, rice and potatoes
- proteins – fish, meat and meat alternatives, such as tofu and soya
- fruit and vegetables – broccoli, leeks, tomatoes, apples and bananas
- dairy – milk, yoghurt, cheese and dairy alternatives, such as oat milk or coconut yoghurt
- oils and spreads – butter, olive oil, vegetable oil and margarine.

Figure 9.1 Examples of healthy foods

All of the foods from the food groups have benefits for the body and help people to stay fit and healthy.
- Carbohydrates give us energy.
- Proteins help our bodies to grow and repair.
- Fruit and vegetables give us vitamins and minerals which help every part of our body to develop and stay healthy, so that we have clear skin, a healthy heart, etc.
- Dairy gives us calcium, which is needed for strong bones and teeth.
- Fats help the body to use all of the fats and minerals where they are needed in the body.

The table on page 89 shows all of the main nutrients that make up a balanced diet, the food that these nutrients can be found in and the benefits for the body.

Nutrient	Food the nutrient is found in	Benefits for the body
Protein	Meat, eggs, fish, milk and other dairy products For vegetarians – wheat, oats, pulses, lentils and soya products, such as Quorn burgers	Helps the body to repair cells Helps the body to grow and develop well
Carbohydrates	Bread, pasta, flour, potatoes, couscous and bananas	Gives the body energy Can help to cut the risk of diseases such as diabetes and heart disease
Fats	Butter, margarine, vegetable oil, other dairy products and fish	Gives the body energy Helps to build healthy cells Helps to keep our brain healthy
Iron	Red meat, broccoli, spinach, egg yolk, plain chocolate and dried fruits	Helps the blood to carry oxygen through the body During pregnancy, the mother's iron helps the baby's brain to develop
Calcium	Milk, cheese, butter, yoghurt, other dairy products, cereals and grains	Good for healthy bones and teeth Helps to keep our heart healthy
Vitamin A	Carrots, milk, apricots, oily fish and margarine	Good for healthy eyes and clear eyesight
Vitamin B	Bread, meat, pasta, flour, rice, noodles and yeast	Good for a healthy nervous system Helps the body to release energy from other food
Vitamin C	Oranges, lemons, grapefruits, blackcurrants, kiwis, potatoes and sweet potatoes	Good for healthy gums and skin Helps to heal cuts Can help treat the common cold
Vitamin E	Vegetable oil, spinach, nuts and wheat germ	Works as an **antioxidant**, protecting the eyes, liver and skin from environmental pollution

Table 9.1 The main nutrients in a balanced diet, the food groups these nutrients are found in and the benefits for the body

Important word

Antioxidant – this works to reverse the damage that pollution has on the body

1.2 The effects on health if a diet is not balanced

If individuals do not eat a balanced diet and do not eat enough of the healthy, nutritious food shown in Table 9.1, their bodies may not develop properly or they may have health problems. If individuals eat too much unhealthy food, such as junk food, crisps and sweets, they may feel a lack of energy, become obese or develop illness and disease.

A balanced diet does not include just food; it also includes what individuals drink each day. For example, sugary drinks can cause teeth to rot and people to gain weight. Energy drinks can be addictive and may cause damage to bodies by speeding up the heart.

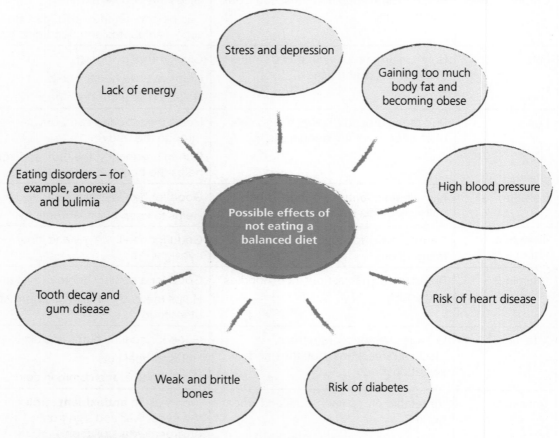

Figure 9.2 Possible effects of not eating a balanced diet

Assessment task 1.1 1.2 1.3

Design a poster that can be displayed at the local doctors' surgery that shows:
◆ what is meant by a balanced diet
◆ the effects on health if a diet is not balanced
◆ ways that food can **contribute to helping an individual stay healthy**.

Important words

Contribute – help to support

Informing individuals – letting people know

1.4 Ways to inform people to eat a balanced diet

Some people do not understand the importance of eating a balanced diet, perhaps because they have never learned about healthy eating or because they do not understand the dangers of eating a poor diet. This means that **informing individuals** about the benefits of eating a healthy diet is very important, so they are healthy and happy.

Ways that people can be informed about healthy diets are:
◆ researching on the internet
◆ watching television programmes about healthy eating
◆ reading books, magazines and leaflets
◆ getting advice from health care workers or nutritionists
◆ joining a club or group interested in healthy weight
◆ being aware of nutrition tables on food packages.

Assessment task 1.4

Make a leaflet about the ways that individuals can get information about eating a balanced diet.

2.1 2.2 The recommended daily fluid intake and how drinking enough can help you to stay healthy

The human body needs enough water and other healthy fluids to stay healthy, work properly and not become **dehydrated**. Water is not just important for stopping us feeling thirsty; we also need water to make our cells work properly. Water also has the job of carrying the important nutrients around the body in the blood and taking away the waste products from our body. It is important for people to drink water and other healthy drinks all through the day to put the fluid back that is lost through sweating, passing urine and even breathing.

Sugary, fizzy drinks, energy drinks and alcohol are not healthy fluids. These types of drinks will make the body lose water and become dehydrated.

Health professionals suggest the following **recommended daily fluid intake**:
◆ Women should drink around 1.5 litres of healthy fluids every day (eight glasses).
◆ Men should drink around 2 litres of healthy fluids every day (ten glasses).

Important words

Dehydrated – dried out and thirsty

Recommended daily fluid intake – the amount of water that experts say we should drink every day

Figure 9.3 It is important for people to drink water throughout the day

2.3 2.4 The signs of not drinking enough and how this can affect health

There are signs that people can feel and see when they are not drinking enough healthy fluids and have become dehydrated.

If dehydration is not treated properly and the lost fluids are not replaced, people can become unwell. If they continue to not drink enough, they may develop long-term illness.

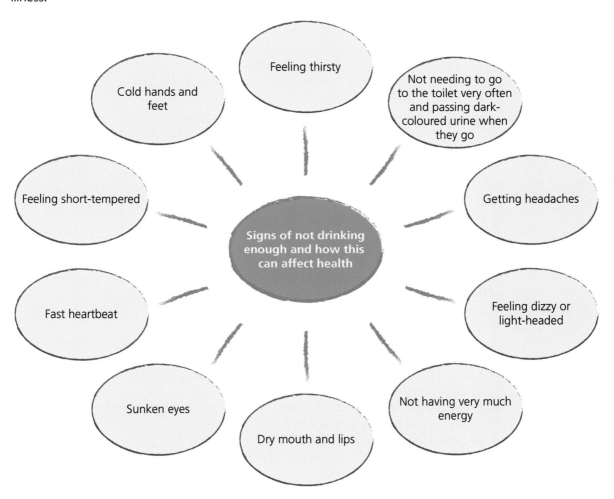

Figure 9.4 Signs of not drinking enough and how this can affect health

Short- and long-term effects to health of not drinking enough:

◆ Heat exhaustion – this can be caused by losing water through sweating and not drinking enough to replace the lost fluids.
◆ Liver damage – caused by not drinking enough fluids.
◆ Kidney problems – kidney stones can grow if a person does not drink enough fluids every day.
◆ Muscle and joint damage – the right levels of fluid in the body are needed to keep muscles and joints working correctly.
◆ Constipation – not being able to empty the bowels of the body's waste due to lack of fluids.
◆ The pulse becomes weak and low blood pressure can also be a problem when a person does not have enough fluids in the body.
◆ A person can become unconscious and vital organs can begin to shut down when the body is lacking in fluids.

Assessment task 2.1 2.2 2.3 2.4

Make an information poster to help people understand the importance of drinking enough to stay healthy. Do some research using books and the internet, and include what you have learned in 2.1–2.4 in this unit.

2.5 Ways to encourage individuals to drink enough to stay healthy

It is important that everyone drinks enough fluids to stay hydrated and healthy. Some of the ways to encourage children and adults to drink fluids include:

◆ having easy access to water from taps or water coolers
◆ carrying a small bottle of water
◆ putting water into child-friendly containers (such as cups with pictures of their favourite characters)
◆ taking a drink of water to the bedroom to drink during the night
◆ offering more drinks during hot weather
◆ offering sugar-free ice lollies to keep cool and hydrated in the summer
◆ offering older aged adults regular drinks
◆ regularly offering babies cool, boiled water
◆ offering a drink with snacks and at meal times.

Figure 9.5 Child-friendly water container

Assessment task 2.5

Megan is seven years old and has recently suffered with very dry lips and mouth. The health visitor has suggested that Megan might not be drinking enough fluids. How can Megan's mum encourage her to drink enough fluids to stay healthy?

Summary

In this unit, you have learned that:

- healthy eating is very important to support growth and development
- a balanced diet is needed to stay healthy
- all people should understand the importance of eating a balanced diet
- people must drink enough healthy fluids to stay hydrated
- there are many signs and symptoms when a person is not drinking enough fluids.

Chapter 10

CFC 15 Human growth and development

What you will learn in this unit

You will gain an understanding of:

◆ the stages of growth and development that people go through
◆ the factors that may affect physical growth and development
◆ the effects of ageing later on in life.

Case study

Grace is 82 years old. She lives alone because her partner died two years ago. Grace has lived an active life but has recently experienced a stroke, so she has had to spend a few weeks in her local hospital. She has made some good progress and, as she is getting better, she is hoping to leave the hospital soon to go home.

Grace's daughter lives nearby, so she will help Grace by cooking her food and doing jobs around the house.

Before Grace leaves the hospital, a specialist nurse must consider how well Grace will be able to manage at home. She needs to find out about Grace's physical, intellectual, **emotional and social well-being**.

Grace has enjoyed swimming all her life and swam twice a week in the local pool as a child and throughout her life until she reached 74 years of age. Grace has always made sure that she eats a good, balanced diet. She admitted to smoking for a couple of years during her teenage years. However, she realised it was unhealthy and soon stopped.

She caught measles when she was seven years old, which made her very ill. Grace has slight hearing loss in one ear because of this illness.

The happiest times in Grace's life were when she married Bob, her partner, and when her children were born. The time when Grace was most sad was when her partner died; she then had to live alone. Another difficult time for Grace was when she experienced the stroke. This made her very frightened and worried about how she would look after herself in the future.

This case study will be referred to later in this chapter.

Important words

Emotional and social well-being – happiness in yourself and as part of a group (society)

Well-being – an individual's good physical and mental health

LO1 Human growth and development

1.1 Main stages of human growth and development

People move through different stages of growth and development during their lives. When we are talking about a person's lifetime, we can look at five important 'life stages', which are shown in Figure 10.1.

Infancy   Childhood   Adolescence   Adulthood   Older adulthood

Figure 10.1 A timeline of the different life stages

Infancy

This is the time between birth and five years. It is a time when young children need their families to provide everything they require, such as food and drink, and to meet their social and communication needs as they are not able to care for themselves yet.

Although some children at this age will not be at school, they are still learning at a very fast rate. During this time, children change from being a tiny baby to a school-aged child who can walk, talk and begin to care for themselves.

Childhood

This is the time in a child's life when they start full-time school and begin to have their own friends. The stage of childhood begins at the age of 5 and continues until a child is about 12 years old.

Again, growth and development are happening quickly and a child changes very much during this stage. Adults should enable the child to try to do more things for themselves, such as helping them to wash and dress themselves, so that as they get older children can learn to care for themselves.

Adolescence

This stage in a person's life begins at around 12 or 13 years of age, as they become a teenager. During this stage, the body goes through many physical changes which are linked to reproduction (having babies). Hormone changes inside the body can affect growth, mood and appearance. Some teenagers find this stage of their life quite difficult, but most of this will have disappeared as they reach adulthood.

Adulthood

When people move into adulthood, they may have a job, a partner and perhaps even a family of their own to care for. Physical growth and development have stopped, and later in adulthood the body begins to show signs of ageing – for example, some adults may not be able to run as fast or climb as many stairs as they used to. However, social and emotional changes are still happening at this stage and the brain is still working very well.

Figure 10.2 Older adulthood brings many challenges, but it can also be a happy and fulfilling time of life

Older adulthood

During this life stage, people are more likely to become ill or physically less able. This is because a person's body is getting weaker, particularly if they did not take care of their bodies when they were teenagers and adults. If we smoke or drink too much alcohol, it could damage our bodies.

During this life stage, skin begins to lose elasticity so will become lined. Hair will lose its colour and become grey. Muscles weaken, so walking may become slower and tasks that were once easy may become difficult.

Some older people might have sight or hearing loss. They may live alone after the death of a partner and their family may not live nearby, so they may become lonely. However, older adults often have lots of wisdom and experience of the world and enjoy their lives very much.

Assessment task 1.1 1.2 2.1

Refer to the case study on page 96. Make a poster to show:
◆ a **pathway** of Grace's life – remember to include all five stages; use pictures from magazines or draw what a person at each stage will look like
◆ a brief description of the effects of ageing that Grace may have experienced during older adulthood
◆ what is meant by physical, intellectual, emotional and social development.

Use the information in the next paragraphs to help you.

Important word

Pathway – a timeline

1.2 What is physical, intellectual, emotional and social development?

Physical development
This means the way in which bodies grow and how people develop physical skills.
◆ A baby learns to walk.
◆ A child will be developing new skills, such as balancing, catching a ball or learning to draw.
◆ A teenager might run quickly and jump over objects.
◆ Adults mostly use the skills they have but sometimes learn new or more difficult skills, such as rock climbing.
As we move into older adulthood, physical skills or activities may become more difficult – for instance, running. As they age, some older adults may need a stick to support them when walking.

Intellectual development
This is the way in which our brain develops and works. As we go through the different life stages, our brain takes in more information that we can understand and use.
◆ Babies are born not knowing much but quickly learn from the people and the world around them.

- Most children learn to read and write, so can understand more and communicate with others to get more information about the world.
- Adults continue to learn and use their knowledge and understanding in their work. However, as we move through older adulthood, the brain may start to slow down and people can become forgetful or confused.

Emotional development

This is the development of many emotions, such as anxiety and fear or excitement and joy. During each life stage, people have different emotions to deal with. Experiencing or feeling these emotions is completely normal.

We are usually aware of why we might feel these emotions, such as feeling confident or nervous when meeting new people or excited at being given or giving someone a present. Children and adults need to develop **resilience** to deal with emotions as these are all part of life.

Social development

This is about understanding the needs of others as well as your own, within social relationships. It is also about understanding how to behave in different places. For example, children need to know how to behave towards teachers and their friends in school, and teenagers have more independence and need to behave in a more mature way.

Children and teenagers need to understand that they can cause others to be upset or worried if they are unkind to each other, but they can also help others to feel good about themselves if they show kindness and support.

Older adults might lose partners or friends that they spent time with, so to stop them becoming lonely they may find new ways to socialise.

Important word

Resilience – being able to cope with a situation or feeling

Task

Think about the emotions that a child starting school might feel. Write down ways in which an adult can help the child to cope with this new experience.

Example!

- A young child might be upset if they lose a favourite toy.
- A teenager may worry about exams or friendships, whereas an adult may worry about household bills.
- An older adult may feel annoyed if they cannot do something which they found easy to do when they were younger.

LO2 Factors affecting growth and development

2.1 Factors affecting physical growth and development

As a person goes through the life stages from birth to older adulthood, there are many **factors** which may affect physical growth. These include

◆ *Exercise* – the amount of exercise an individual does each day can affect physical growth and development. This is because our body needs the benefits of physical activity, such as increased heart rate, improved **stamina** to develop strong muscles, healthy bones and maintaining a healthy body weight. Exercise helps our body to develop because when we exercise regularly we sleep better, which also supports healthy growth and development.

◆ *Diet* – the food and drinks we choose affect our growth and development in an important way. This is because different foods have different health benefits; some foods give us the vitamins and minerals that our body needs to stay healthy, and other foods contain too much fat or sugar which, when we eat them too often, can lead to illness, such as diabetes.

◆ *Illness* – when we are ill, our body may become weak and perhaps feel very tired, so we may not want to eat healthily or do any exercise.

◆ *Lifestyle* – this means the choices we make during our life, such as what we choose to eat and drink, the way we spend our time and the amount of exercise and sleep we have each day.

Important words

Factors – negative or positive things that may have happened

Stamina – the strength and energy people need to do physical activity

Lifestyle – way of life

2.2 Life events which can affect emotional and social well-being

There are certain times in a person's life, called **life events**, that can affect their emotional and social well-being.

◆ Good experiences that can make an adult feel happy may include a birth in the family, getting married, getting a good job or moving to a new house.

◆ There could also be times in an adult's life when they feel sad or very worried, such as losing a home or a job, a family splitting up or the death of a close family member.

Important words

Life event – something that has happened to a person that has affected their life, such as serious illness or loss of a family member

Figure 10.3 A wedding is an important life event

Task

Think about different events or factors that have affected your physical health and experiences, and your emotional and social well-being.

Assessment task 2.1 2.2

Think about the case study on page 96.

Using what you have learned about Grace:
◆ list three factors which may have affected her physical health and development during her lifetime
◆ list three experiences which may have affected her emotional and social well-being.

2.3 The effects of ageing in the later stages of life

You have already covered some of the effects of older adulthood on pages 98-99.

During late adulthood, a person's mobility, such as walking and balance, might not be as good as when they were younger, so trips and falls are more common. A person in late adulthood may be slower to react to dangers – for example, when crossing a road, an older aged adult may not be able to move more quickly if a fast car is approaching.

It is common for a person's hearing and eyesight to become poorer in the later stages of life. This can make a person feel afraid of going out alone if they have poor eyesight, or lonely if they have poor hearing and cannot join in conversations.

Memory can also become poor in the later stages of life, so older adults find it harder to remember information, such as appointment times or daily care routines, for example, whether they have taken their medicine today.

During this life stage, people are more likely to become ill because an older aged adult has a weaker immune system, which is how the body fights disease and infections. A person in the later stages of life will probably need more support to care for themselves and to carry on taking part in activities they enjoy.

Assessment task 2.3

Write down three effects that ageing may have on an older aged adult.

Research on the internet to find another effect of ageing for older aged adults.

In small groups, think about an older person that you know (it could be a neighbour or grandparent). Discuss the effects that ageing has had on this person.

You could also write down ways that family or friends could help this older person to continue to safely care for themselves – for example, having handrails fitted for outdoor steps.

Summary

In this unit, you have learned that:

- there are five main life stages
- factors such as diet, lifestyle and exercise can affect physical growth and development
- events such as the birth of a child or the death of a close family member are called 'life events'
- life events can affect a person's social and emotional well-being.

Chapter 11

INTRO MU 1.7 Introduction to children's and young people's development

What you will learn in this unit

You will gain an understanding of:

◆ the stages of children's and young people's development (0–19 years)
◆ the factors that affect children's and young people's development
◆ ways to support children's and young people's development.

LO1 The main stages of children's and young people's development

1.1 The expected pattern of development for children and young people (0–19 years)

During the time between birth and 19 years, a person will change from being **dependent** on their parents or carers, who will have to meet all of their care needs, to becoming **independent**, able to look after themselves and manage their own lives.

There are four main areas of development:

◆ language and communication
◆ physical development
◆ intellectual development
◆ personal, social and emotional development.

Important words

Dependent – needing the help and support of others

Independent – not always needing the help and support of others

Language and communication

At first, a baby is only able to cry, but quickly learns to make cooing and gurgling sounds. During the first year of life, a baby will begin to understand simple words, such as their own name and the name of a pet.

At this age, babies enjoy listening to songs and rhymes and, by the age of 12 months, they know and can say one or two words and copy sounds.

Physical development

At birth, a baby has reflexes such as sucking and grasping. A baby soon begins to control their body – for example, using their hands to move objects or pull things towards them.

At around 8 months, a baby will begin to sit without support and may start to crawl. Babies will begin to hold finger foods and drink from a trainer cup with handles.

Around 11 months, a child may stand holding on to furniture or even take their first steps.

Personal, social and emotional development

A baby will cry when in pain, hungry or uncomfortable, such as when they have a wet nappy or feel too hot or cold.

By the age of 3 months, a baby may copy an adult's smile and will know the difference between family members. A baby usually enjoys contact with family members, such as when feeding and being bathed.

At around 9 months, babies may become clingy with family members because they are now more aware of strangers.

Intellectual development

A new baby begins to use senses to hear, smell and see what is going on around them.

From around 6 months, babies enjoy playing, moving toys and objects from one place to another. By the time they are 12 months old, they are able to stack one brick on to another. Babies enjoy looking at bright colours.

Figure 11.1 Expected patterns of development from birth to 12 months

Language and communication

Children begin to repeat a few words around the age of 14 months and understand some instructions, such as 'coat on' and 'come here'.

A child will put three or four words together to make sentences – for example, 'me do that' or 'little dog barking'.

Children will learn lots of new words and enjoy looking at picture books and listening to stories. By the age of 3 years, they will understand around 600 words.

Physical development

At 12 months, children can usually stand without support and begin to walk. They start to climb up stairs, so need to be watched!

By the age of 2 years, a child can run, throw and kick a ball.

By the time children are 3 years old, they have usually learned to jump off a low step and may ride a tricycle. They may also use a spoon and fork properly when feeding themselves.

Personal, social and emotional development

A child may be interested in looking at themselves in the mirror. Children enjoy playing with other children and adults.

By 3 years of age, children understand the meaning of different facial expressions – for example, a child will know when a person is happy or sad.

Intellectual development

Children begin to enjoy playing – moving toys and objects from one place to another so that by the time the child is 18 months old, they are able to stack three or four bricks in a tower.

Children may enjoy playdough and messy activities. As children get older, they may enjoy listening to others count and may begin to join in. They may also enjoy listening to stories and know the names of the characters in their favourite stories.

Figure 11.2 Expected patterns of development from 12 months to 3 years

Language and communication

By 4 years, children can understand over 1000 words and make sentences of five or more words.

Children now enjoy listening to longer stories and will often choose the same story over and over again.

Children at 5 years know up to 2000 words and use proper sentences. Children often talk clearly and will enjoy telling stories about themselves.

Physical development

Children can stand on one leg, and jump up and down. At this age, children enjoy climbing and can change direction quickly when running in the play area.

They may now be able to take responsibility for their own toileting. They can open and close fastenings, and can dress and undress for a PE lesson.

Children can use scissors to cut out shapes and pictures. They can skip with a rope, and can run quickly and safely around the playground without bumping into other children.

Personal, social and emotional development

At this age, children like to spend time playing alone but also enjoy playing with other children. They may enjoy caring for pets. At 4 years, children show concern when a friend is hurt.

Children will like to make choices for themselves, such as deciding which clothes to wear or what book to look at.

Children at 5 years usually enjoy being busy and playing co-operatively. This means that they can agree rules of a game and take turns.

Intellectual development

By the age of 3 years, children begin to enjoy counting up to ten and learning the names of colours and shapes.

At the age of 4, children may copy letters and numbers and may write their own name. They may know the names of most colours and most simple shapes.

At the age of 5 years, children may draw pictures of trees, houses, people and animals, and complete a 20-piece jigsaw puzzle.

Figure 11.3 Expected patterns of development from 3–5 years

Language and communication

During this time, children become more and more independent and, as they get older, will possibly spend less time with their families, as they want to spend time with friends.

Children can agree rules during play, and will give and take instructions.

Children can read the body language of other people and can understand how someone feels by their tone of voice.

Physical development

At this age, children's balance and co-ordination improve. They can become very skilled in an activity or sport, such as ballet or football.

Up to the age of 11 years, children will be able to gain more difficult skills using their hands, such as knitting, model making and building with small bricks.

Children will begin to be able to care for themselves physically, such as washing their own hair and cleaning their teeth.

Personal, social and emotional development

Between the ages of 5 and 11 years, children are developing social skills and learning how to work together with others. As they get older, children are able to see things from the other person's point of view when having a discussion.

Children at this age are very aware of social rules and how to behave; they will understand what may happen when they break any rules.

Intellectual development

Children at primary school will be developing mathematical skills such as adding up and taking away numbers.

Children will learn how to tell the time, and will understand about seasons and changes in the weather.

Older children will be able to do more complicated maths problems and will be developing a good understanding of the world around them.

Figure 11.4 Expected patterns of development from 5–11 years

Language and communication

Young people will use their communication skills to put across their own views and opinions.

Some young people at this age find it more and more difficult to communicate with parents and adults in authority, such as teachers. They often find it easier to communicate with others who are their own age.

Physical development

There are many physical changes taking place during this stage, which is known as adolescence. Bodies go through changes linked to reproduction. Hormones affect growth of bones and muscles, mood and appearance, such as hair growth.

Girls will develop breasts and their periods will begin during this stage. Boys' voices deepen and they may begin to shave.

Personal, social and emotional development

Some adolescents find this time to be emotionally difficult as they get used to the changes in their bodies and they become more like adults.

Young people usually want to be more independent during this stage and this can sometimes cause arguments in families.

During this time, girls and boys may have relationships which can be special to them but may also cause problems for them emotionally.

Intellectual development

Young people are very aware of the world around them and understand how things work. Many young people are skilled at using a computer or are very interested in one or more of the subjects they learn about in school.

Young people will often start to take an interest in the wider world, such as listening to world news or what is happening in their local area.

Figure 11.5 Expected patterns of development from 11–19 years

Assessment task 1.1

Design a wall display which shows the **expected pattern of development** for children and young people aged 0–19 years. Include:
◆ language and communication
◆ physical development
◆ intellectual development
◆ personal, social and emotional development.

Important words

Expected pattern of development – the order in which most people develop

LO2 The factors that affect children's and young people's development

2.1 Factors that affect children and young people's development

There are a number of factors that can affect children's growth and development, including their background, health and environment.

Background

A child or young person's background, including their personal history (this is what has happened in their lives so far), such as loss of a parent or unhealthy lifestyle choices, affects their development. Culture and religious beliefs may also affect social development, as some children and young people are expected only to mix in their own groups.

Language development

Language development is mostly affected by the way that children are spoken to and communicated with when they are young. If a child is encouraged to talk and is included in conversations – for example, asking the child what they did when they went to nursery or asking them about pictures in a book – it will support their language development.

Children copy what they hear, so it is very important for young people and adults to only use appropriate language around a young child. If a child hears others using swear words or saying unkind things, the child will copy this and they might use this language when they are at school. This could get them into trouble, which may upset the child. Adults should be good role models for young children, especially when working in health and social care and childcare.

Family relationships

The family can have a big effect on a child or young person's development. If the child spends time with members of their family, playing games, reading stories or going out to places, their development will be supported.

For example, if a child goes shopping with family members, they will be seeing the world around them and learning new things; they might also see how to communicate well. If parents or carers are responsible carers, giving time to their children and showing them care and kindness, this can support children's development.

If, however, a child or young person does not have the chance to spend good quality time with family members they may not understand about good trusting relationships, they may not have their care needs met and they may not feel secure. This can affect their development.

Health

Health can be affected by the choices a person makes, by the environment or by their physical health. It includes diet, exercise, illness and disability.

Diet

A good, well-balanced diet will help to support children's healthy growth and development.

A poor diet might mean that children and young people are not getting all the vitamins and nutrients they need to keep their bodies healthy. They may also have too much salt, fat or sugar in their diet, which could cause health problems.

Figure 11.6 Eating fruit as part of a well-balanced diet

Exercise

Exercise gives children and young people the chance to use their muscles to become strong, flexible and healthy.

Not having enough exercise might cause muscles to become weak. Children may build up too much body fat and become ill later in life.

Figure 11.7 Hula hooping can help to build a strong and healthy body

Illness

Illness can affect growth and development. Some illnesses can mean that a child may stop growing or grow very slowly.

Illness affects a child's or young person's development as they may spend time in hospital or be unable to go to school to learn and to meet with their friends. They may not be able to develop intellectually (learn new things) or develop good social skills.

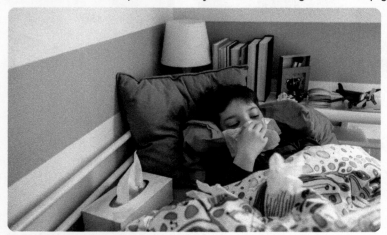

Figure 11.8 Too ill to go to school

Disability

Disability may affect a child's or young person's development if they are not given the correct support from adults. For example, a child who needs glasses might not be able to see pictures in a book or the computer screen clearly.

However, if a young person using a wheelchair is given the correct support, he or she should be able to enjoy most activities with others.

Environment

The environment – or the world around a child or young person – can affect their development.

Lifestyle

The lifestyle of the family can have a good or bad effect on the child's or young person's development. If adults smoke in the house, close to where the child or young person is sleeping or playing, they could have some breathing difficulties or hearing problems known as 'glue ear'.

Figure 11.9 Support from adults is important

Money

The amount of money a family has can affect a child or young person. For example, if there is not enough money to buy warm clothes or to go on trips and visits, the child's development might be affected.

Housing

If the child has lots of space to run and play outdoors, they will have more opportunities to develop physically. However, if they live in an area where it is not very safe to play outdoors – for example, they live beside a busy road or in a tall block of flats – they might not have the chance to play outdoors so often.

A young person might live next to noisy neighbours and might not get a good amount of sleep each night, so their intellectual development may be affected if they cannot concentrate at school. If the house is crowded, there might not be a quiet place to do homework, so again intellectual development might be affected compared to a young person who has a quite area to study at home.

Employment

Employment can also have an effect on a child's development. This is because if the parents work, the child might go to a day nursery or an other childcare setting, and the quality of this care will affect the child's development.

Assessment task 2.1

Make a poster showing the different factors that can affect children's growth and development, including:
- background
- health
- environment.

LO3 How to support children's and young people's development

3.1 Different ways to support children's and young people's development

Children and young people need help and support to develop. There are many ways that this help and support can be given within the four main areas of development. Some ways include the following:

- *Physical development* can be supported by giving children and young people the opportunity to take part in physical activities such as sports or craft activities.
- *Personal, social and emotional development* can be supported by giving children and young people the opportunity to take part in group activities or to enjoy being part of a team. Giving children and young people clear rules, such as agreeing classroom rules or being told the rules of a game, will support them to understand expected behaviour.
- *Language and communication* can be supported by taking time to talk to children and young people and giving them the opportunity to join in with group discussions. Sharing books and stories with young children is a good way to help them to learn new words.
- *Intellectual development* can be supported by giving children and young people the opportunity to learn new things and to explore the world around them. It is important that adults encourage children and young people to ask questions when they don't understand things because this helps them to develop good understanding.

Task

Using what you have learned about children's and young people's development, complete the following diagrams suggesting ways to support children and young people's development.

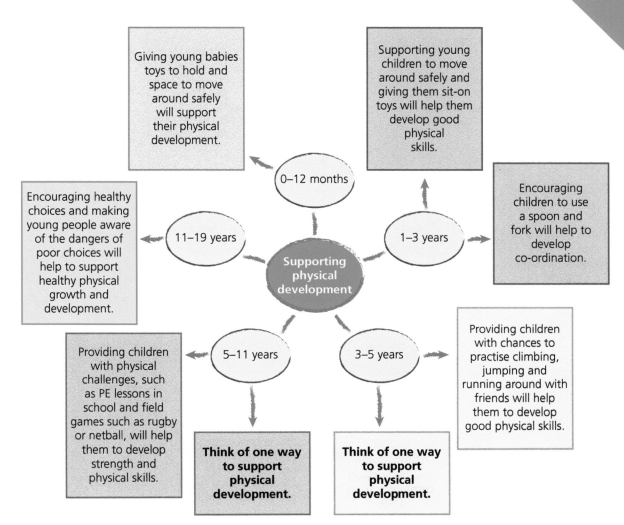

Figure 11.10 Supporting physical development

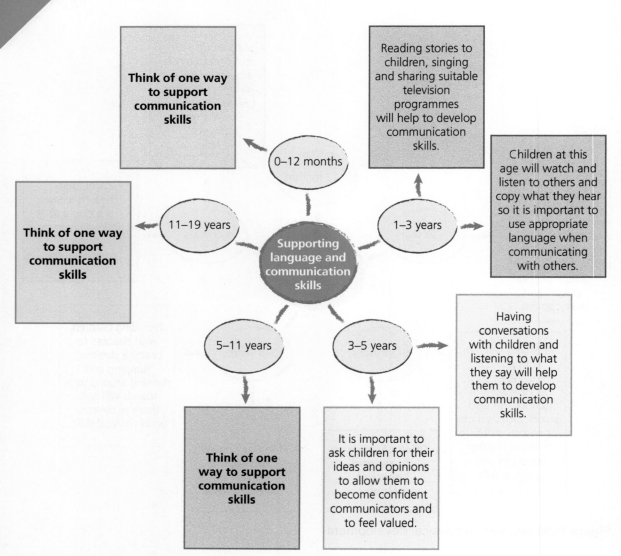

Figure 11.11 Supporting language and communication skills

The following text appears within the figure:

Think of one way to support communication skills

0–12 months

Reading stories to children, singing and sharing suitable television programmes will help to develop communication skills.

1–3 years

Children at this age will watch and listen to others and copy what they hear so it is important to use appropriate language when communicating with others.

Think of one way to support communication skills

11–19 years

Supporting language and communication skills

5–11 years

3–5 years

Having conversations with children and listening to what they say will help them to develop communication skills.

Think of one way to support communication skills

It is important to ask children for their ideas and opinions to allow them to become confident communicators and to feel valued.

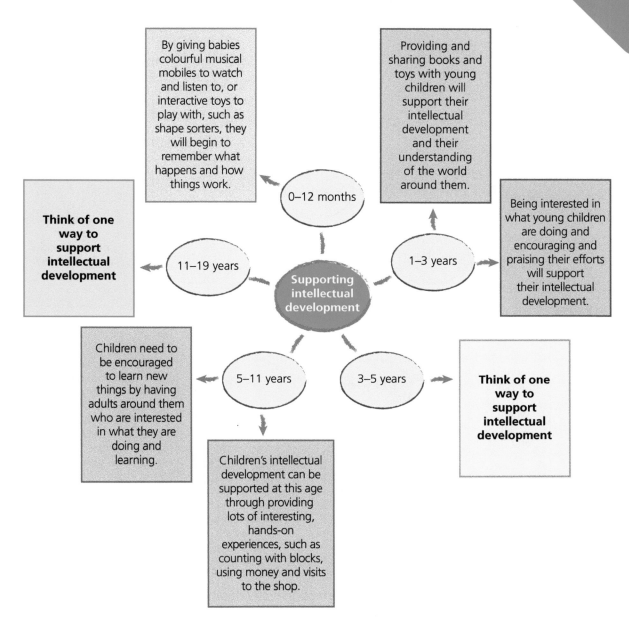

By giving babies colourful musical mobiles to watch and listen to, or interactive toys to play with, such as shape sorters, they will begin to remember what happens and how things work.

Providing and sharing books and toys with young children will support their intellectual development and their understanding of the world around them.

Think of one way to support intellectual development

Being interested in what young children are doing and encouraging and praising their efforts will support their intellectual development.

0–12 months

11–19 years

Supporting intellectual development

1–3 years

Children need to be encouraged to learn new things by having adults around them who are interested in what they are doing and learning.

5–11 years

3–5 years

Think of one way to support intellectual development

Children's intellectual development can be supported at this age through providing lots of interesting, hands-on experiences, such as counting with blocks, using money and visits to the shop.

Figure 11.12 Supporting intellectual development

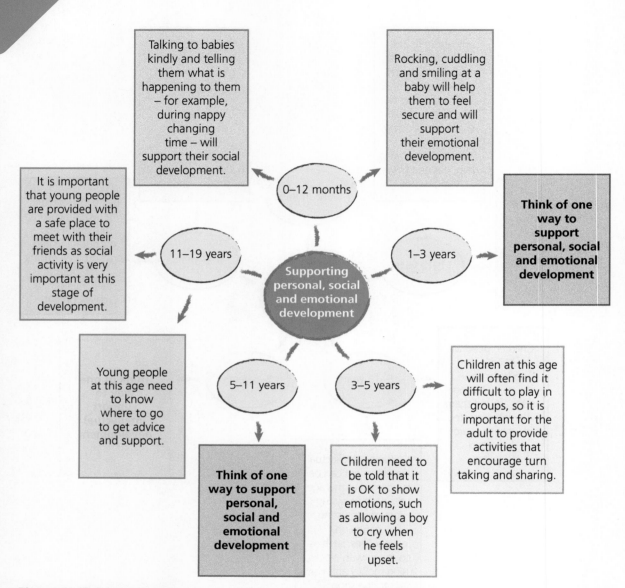

Figure 11.13 Supporting personal, social and emotional development

Assessment task 3.1

Adding to your wall display, include information about the different ways to support children's and young people's development. Include a minimum of two examples for each of the following areas:
◆ physical development
◆ language and communication
◆ intellectual development
◆ personal, social and emotional development.

Summary

In this unit, you have learned that:
◆ children and young people aged 0–19 years go through several main stages of development
◆ there are many factors that affect children's and young people's development
◆ there are many ways to support children's and young people's development.

Chapter 12

INTRO OP 1.1 Understand the importance of engagement in leisure and social activities in health and social care

What you will learn in this unit

You will gain an understanding of:

◆ the importance of leisure and social activities for an individual's well-being

◆ how leisure and social activities support relationships

◆ a range of leisure and social activities

◆ how to find out about the interests and preferences of individuals

◆ the benefits of a person-centred approach for individuals taking part in leisure or social activities

◆ the different types of support that individuals may need so they can take part in leisure and social activities

◆ how to promote independence through leisure and social activities.

LO1 Why leisure and social activities are important for an individual's well-being and relationships

1.1 1.2 Why leisure and social activities are important for an individual's well-being and support relationships

Everybody needs to spend time relaxing and doing things that they enjoy, either on their own or with friends. **Leisure activities** give children and adults the chance to take part in activities that interest them and help them to relax. For example, children may enjoy riding their bike in the local park, families may enjoy walks together and older aged adults may enjoy attending clubs or going on day trips.

These sorts of activities are very important for an individual's **well-being** because they help to create a fit and healthy body and also boost mental well-being, helping people feel more positive and relaxed.

Children and adults may spend time enjoying leisure activities with other individuals or groups. For example, a child may visit the local park with friends from school and an older aged adult may belong to a walking club which meets every weekend to walk together as a group. Taking part in **social activities** or hobbies helps to **support relationships** because people have the chance to make new friends and also to enjoy friendships with people that they already know.

Family leisure activities allow families to strengthen their relationships and spend quality time together.

> ## Important words
>
> **Leisure activities** – interests or hobbies that people can enjoy
>
> **Well-being** – an individual's good physical and mental health
>
> **Social activities** – activities that people take part in with others
>
> **Support relationships** – spending time with others to strengthen friendships and meet new people

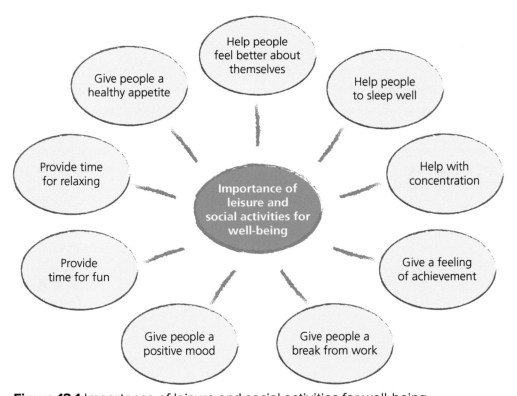

Figure 12.1 Importance of leisure and social activities for well-being

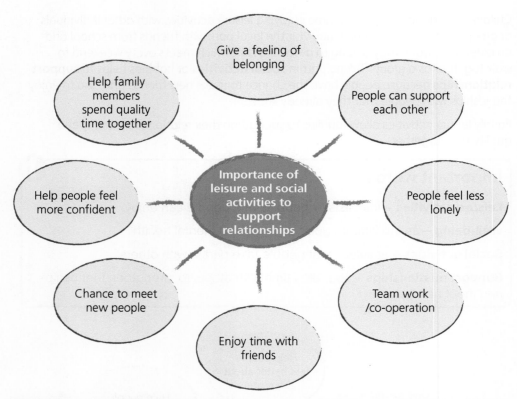

Figure 12.2 Importance of leisure and social activities to support relationships

LO2 A range of leisure and social activities

2.1 Identify a range of leisure and social activities that take place within:

◆ a person's own home
◆ a local community
◆ a residential or group living home
◆ day care provision.

There are many different leisure and social activities that can be enjoyed by children and adults, whether in their own home, in different health and social care settings or within the local community.

Figure 12.3 A family enjoying a bike trip

Place of leisure or social activity	Leisure or social activity			
A person's home	A party with friends	Reading a book or watching a film	Coffee and cake mornings with neighbours and friends	Gardening
A local community	Football club	Singing in the local choir	Swimming club	Craft fair
A residential or group living home	Playing board games	Group trip to the seaside	Watching old films	Visit from family and friends
Day care provision	Sewing and knitting groups	Flower arranging	Sing-a-longs	Lunch clubs

Table 12.1 Different social and leisure activities and where they can take place

Assessment task 2.1

Make your own table like Table 12.1 to show two other leisure and social activities that can take place in:
- a local community
- a person's own home
- a residential home
- day care provision.

LO3 How a person-centred approach supports individuals in leisure or social activities

3.1 How to find out about the interests and preferences of individuals

There are many ways to find out about the **interests and preferences** of individuals and these include:

◆ asking a person about their interests
◆ giving a person choices
◆ using questionnaires or suggestion boxes
◆ talking to families and carers
◆ observing a person's enjoyment of different activities
◆ looking at personal records
◆ providing a range of leisure and social activities to give a person choices.

> **Important words**
>
> **Interests and preferences** – the things that a person enjoys and chooses to do

Assessment task 3.1

Ahmed is 20 years old and has learning difficulties. He will be attending a day care centre for two days each week.

How can the carers working in the centre find out about Ahmed's interests and preferences?

3.2 The benefits for individuals of a person-centred approach when taking part in leisure or social activities

Taking the **person-centred approach** will make it easier to provide leisure and social activities that a person enjoys. This is because the interests and preferences of individuals come first.

This is different from not having a person-centred approach where, for example, in a care home a few activities may be provided by the care workers, even if the residents are not very interested in that type of activity.

It is important to take time to find out about a person's interests, likes and dislikes by listening to them, observing them or getting information from others. This information should be used to plan and provide suitable activities for the person, meaning a person-centred approach is being used.

By taking a person-centred approach when planning activities, carers will be able to make sure that the activity is safe for the individual.

There are many benefits to using a person-centred approach when providing leisure and social activities. These may include the following:

◆ A person will want to take part in the activity.
◆ A person will feel happy when the activity is something that they enjoy.
◆ The person may feel good about themselves if they do well in the activity.
◆ The person might make friends with others who enjoy the same activity.
◆ The person may have skills to share with others.
◆ The person's own skills might improve.
◆ The activity will be safe for that person.

Important words

Person-centred approach – understanding a person's individual needs and caring for them in the way that suits them best

---

Assessment task 3.2

Ahmed has now settled into the day care centre and is taking part in the activities. The carers have used a person-centred approach to planning and providing the activities. How will Ahmed benefit from this approach?

3.3 The different types of support that individuals may need to take part in leisure and social activities

There are many types of support that may be needed when individuals take part in leisure or social activities. It may be that an individual needs help to get somewhere, such as to a community or sports centre to take part in an activity. This support could mean someone drives them to the centre or perhaps walks with them if it is close by.

When the person is at the community or sports centre, they may have the support of an instructor or group leader, and they may also get support from others taking part in the activity.

When a person is less able to do things for themselves, they may need a care worker to set out the activity or to support them to take part. For example, if individuals in a residential home for older aged adults are enjoying a dancing session, a person in a wheelchair may enjoy being taken around the dance floor by a carer so they can join in.

Figure 12.4 Taking part in a dancing session

Assessment task 3.3

Describe the different types of support that individuals may need to take part in leisure and social activities within:
- the community
- their own home
- a residential home.

3.4 How to promote independence through leisure and social activities

It is important that care workers allow individuals to be as independent as possible so that they don't lose their skills, or stop trying to do things for themselves. To promote independence through activities, it is important to:

◆ let the person choose their own activities
◆ only give support that the person asks for
◆ let the person know you are there to help when needed
◆ take an interest and join in, without taking over
◆ take notice and praise them when they do well or try hard.

Assessment task 3.4

Read the list above and, in small groups, make a list of other ways to promote independence through leisure and social activities.

Summary

In this unit, you have learned:

◆ the importance of leisure and social activities for an individual's well-being
◆ how leisure and social activities support relationships
◆ that there are many different leisure and social activities
◆ how to find out about the interests and preferences of individuals
◆ the benefits of a person-centred approach for individuals taking part in leisure or social activities
◆ the different types of support that individuals may need to take part in leisure and social activities
◆ how to promote independence through leisure and social activities.

Chapter 13

INTRO OP 1.2 Introduction to a healthy lifestyle

What you will learn in this unit

You will gain an understanding of:

◆ what contributes to a healthy lifestyle
◆ how activities contribute to a healthy lifestyle
◆ what contributes to an unhealthy lifestyle
◆ the positive and negative parts of your own lifestyle
◆ developing a personal healthy lifestyle plan.

LO1 What contributes to a healthy lifestyle

1.1 Factors that contribute to a healthy lifestyle

The main factors that **contribute** to a healthy lifestyle include:

◆ diet
◆ exercise
◆ work and play
◆ rest and sleep.

> ### Important word
>
> **Contribute** – help to support

1.2 Benefits of living a healthy lifestyle

Diet

The food and drink that we take into our bodies have an effect on our health. This means it is important to eat a wide variety of healthy foods in the right amounts to have a healthy body weight. We must also drink lots of healthy fluids to keep our bodies hydrated. We need to eat a good balanced diet that contains all the nutrients needed for growth and good health.

Eating too much food or having a poor diet, such as eating lots of takeaway food which is high in fat and salt, or having too many sugary drinks, can make us overweight. Not eating enough good foods, such as fruit, vegetables and wholegrains, can leave us feeling tired and unable to fight off illness.

Figure 13.1 Healthy foods

Exercise

Regular exercise plays an important part in keeping us healthy; this is because when we move our bodies and exercise we use energy to burn calories and body fat, and muscles become toned and strong.

Regular exercise, such as walking or playing sports, can help us to relax and sleep well. It also helps the body to fight diseases such as diabetes and high blood pressure. Exercise helps us to have a healthy body weight and a positive mind. Exercise, as well as being fun, also **releases** chemicals in our bodies that help to put us into a good mood and to relax.

Important word

Releases – frees

Work and play

Work and play can both support a healthy lifestyle. For example, if a person works regularly they will need to be in a routine where they get out of bed and get ready for work. When working, people will be using their skills and perhaps learning new skills. The type of work a person does might mean that they have to work as part of a team or perhaps make decisions for themselves; this may help to develop confidence or improve communication skills.

Play happens differently for people of different ages – for example, a child may enjoy building sandcastles on the beach, a young person may enjoy playing football with friends on the beach and adults may enjoy walking along the beach. Both work and play can make a person feel proud that they have achieved something or completed a task well.

When a person is out of work, they may feel bored or suffer low self-esteem. When a person does not take part in play activities, they may not have chance to relax and have fun.

Rest and sleep

Sleep is important for us because this is the time when bodies grow and repair themselves; sleep allows us to fight off infection and disease. When we sleep, we store memories and make sense of the world around us.

When we have had enough sleep we are able to concentrate for longer and remember things more clearly. A good night's sleep leaves us feeling fresh and full of energy, ready for the day ahead.

Figure 13.2 A good night's sleep leaves us feeling fresh and full of energy

Assessment task 1.1 1.2

Write a page for a health magazine to give information about healthy lifestyles, including:

◆ the factors that contribute to a healthy lifestyle
◆ the benefits of a healthy lifestyle.

LO2 How activities contribute to a healthy lifestyle

2.1 Activities in the local area that support a healthy lifestyle

Examples of activities that you might find in your local area:

◆ swimming
◆ football
◆ yoga
◆ tennis
◆ basketball
◆ netball
◆ bowling
◆ aerobics classes
◆ dance classes
◆ judo
◆ walking and running.

Figure 13.3 Exercising with weights

Figure 13.4 Tennis

2.2 2.3 The benefits of selected activities on personal well-being

There are many benefits of taking part in activities that support a healthy lifestyle. The benefits can be physical, such as strengthening muscles and fighting infection, and emotional, such as enjoying spending time with friends or feeling good about doing well in the activity.

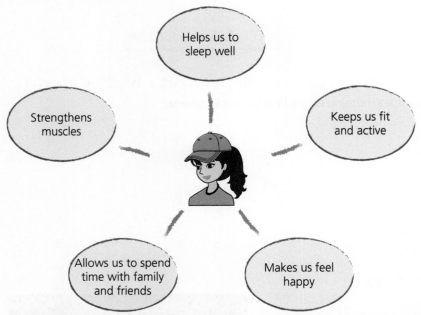

Figure 13.5 The benefits of taking part in activities that support a healthy lifestyle

Assessment task 2.1 2.2 2.3

On your page for the health magazine, list three activities in your local area and write about the benefits of these activities for a person's well-being.

LO3 What contributes to an unhealthy lifestyle

3.1 Activities and choices that hinder a healthy lifestyle

There are a few activities and choices that **hinder** us from having a healthy lifestyle, and we should try to avoid these as much as we can.

Important word

Hinder – stop

Activities and choices to avoid include:
- smoking
- using drugs
- drinking too much alcohol or having too many energy drinks
- eating a poor diet
- unsafe outdoor swimming
- spending too much time on social media or gaming
- lack of exercise
- lack of sleep.

3.2 How these activities and choices can have a negative effect on personal well-being

There are many ways that making poor choices and leading an unhealthy lifestyle can have a negative effect on personal well-being. Eating an unhealthy diet or not exercising enough may mean that we develop too much body fat, feel tired or become unwell. Lack of sleep may make us feel irritable or unable to concentrate properly.

Smoking, drinking too much alcohol and using drugs all damage our body, and can cause illness and disease.

Assessment task 3.1 3.2

On your page for the health magazine:
- list at least three choices or activities that can stop a person from having a healthy lifestyle
- say how these choices or activities could negatively affect the body.

LO4 How to develop a personal healthy lifestyle plan

4.1 Identifying positive and negative aspects of your own lifestyle

We all make choices about our lifestyle, and these choices affect our physical and emotional well-being. For example, if we eat too many takeaway meals, we could be having too much sugar and salt, and not getting the right nutrients to keep us healthy. If we drink too many energy drinks, we risk damaging our bodies and may find it difficult to concentrate.

Each day we make choices that affect our physical and emotional well-being without thinking about it. For example, we may take the lift instead of using the stairs or choose water instead of a sugary drink. All of these choices will have an effect on our health and well-being.

4.2 Producing an action plan to improve own health and well-being

It is important that we all try to have a healthy lifestyle. This means that we have to make the right choices. When we know our usual choices are not the best ones for our health and well-being, it is important that we change what we usually choose to do.

Assessment task 4.1 4.2

Complete the table below to show the positive and negative aspects of your own lifestyle, and ways to make healthy changes.

Positive and negative aspects of my lifestyle	Activities and choices that will improve my health and well-being
I spend too much time on social media and gaming on the computer.	I will only spend two hours each day on social media and gaming. After two hours, I will go outside for fresh air and find another activity to do.
I always walk the dog in the park after dinner.	I will continue to take the dog for a walk because I know this exercise is helping me to stay healthy.

Table 13.1 Ways to make healthy changes

Summary

In this unit, you have learned that:

- some activities and choices help us to have a healthy lifestyle
- some activities and choices mean we have an unhealthy lifestyle
- we can look at the positive and negative aspects of our own lifestyles and make a plan to help us get fitter and healthier.

Chapter 14

What you will learn in this unit

You will gain an understanding of:

- what is meant by 'Autistic Spectrum Condition'
- how to support the individual needs of a person with Autistic Spectrum Condition
- the importance of communicating in a way which best suits individuals with Autistic Spectrum Condition.

LO1 The concept of Autistic Spectrum Condition

1.1 What is 'Autistic Spectrum Condition'?

Autistic Spectrum Condition, sometimes called autism, is a lifelong disability that mostly affects a person's understanding of the world around them and how they communicate with others.

Figure 14.1 People with Autistic Spectrum Condition often find it difficult to communicate with others

1.2 Examples of behavioural characteristics of individuals with Autistic Spectrum Condition

People with Autistic Spectrum Condition look the same as everyone else; however, Autistic Spectrum Condition is a disability. People with Autistic Spectrum Condition see the world differently to others and often have difficulties in taking part in everyday activities, such as school, work or developing friendships.

Autistic Spectrum Condition sometimes causes an individual to carry out the same actions over and over again – for example, opening and closing a door or drawer many times.

Most people with Autistic Spectrum Condition like to have routines which do not change so they know what will happen next. When a routine changes, some people with Autistic Spectrum Condition do not cope well and become upset or frustrated. This can result in challenging behaviour or outbursts of anger.

Example!

I am Lily, I am seven years old and I have Autistic Spectrum Condition …

These are my **behavioural characteristics**:
◆ I have difficulty communicating with my family and friends.
◆ I often get upset or angry when people don't understand what I need or want.
◆ I like my routines to stay the same.
◆ Loud noises upset me.
◆ I find it difficult to make friends because of my communication difficulties.
◆ I am not as good at reading and writing as my friends.
◆ I am amazing at drawing pictures of animals!

Important words

Behavioural characteristics – the types of behaviour a person shows

1.3 Sensory difficulties which may affect individuals with Autistic Spectrum Condition

Sensory difficulties are difficulties which can affect touch, smell, taste, sight and hearing.

Lily's sensory difficulties affect her in many different ways:

Touch	Lily does not like the feel of cotton wool and velvet fabrics. If Lily touches either of these materials, she can become very upset and it is difficult to calm her down. Lily likes playing with water and sand.
Smell	Lily cannot cope with some smells, such as perfumes or air fresheners. These smells make Lily feel anxious and scared.
Taste	There are some tastes Lily dislikes – for example, mashed potato. To stop her from becoming upset, Lily's mum and dad make sure she is not given this food to eat.
Sight	Lily avoids making eye contact with others but will spend time staring at flashing images or lights on her tablet. When Lily draws, she usually uses dark-coloured pencils.
Hearing	Lily has sensitive hearing, which means loud or high-pitched sounds can hurt her ears.

Table 14.1 Lily's sensory difficulties

Figure 14.2 Lily does not like loud noises

Important words

Sensory difficulties – difficulties individuals have when using one or more of the five senses (touch, smell, taste, sight, hearing)

Assessment task 1.1 1.2 1.3

Draw a picture of Lily and write down how having Autistic Spectrum Condition affects her behaviour. Include three sensory difficulties that Lily has.

1.4 The importance of preparation, planning and routines for individuals with Autistic Spectrum Condition

When working with children and adults with disability, it is always important for the practitioner to understand what they like and enjoy doing, and what they dislike and have difficulty with. To make sure the needs of a person with Autistic Spectrum Condition are met and they can enjoy being part of the group, practitioners must prepare and plan activities and care routines carefully.

Practitioners need to think about the things that upset a person with Autistic Spectrum Condition so that they can plan to avoid these things. For example, loud noises hurt Lily's ears and upset her, so practitioners do not plan to test the fire alarm when Lily is in the building.

Assessment task 1.4

You have been asked to plan a creative activity that Lily would enjoy. Think about Lily's sensory difficulties and make sure the planned activity does not include anything that would upset her.

LO2 The importance of a person-centred approach when working with individuals with an Autistic Spectrum Condition

2.1 The importance of recognising and valuing an individual with Autistic Spectrum Condition as a person first

When working with a children and adults, it is important that practitioners get to know them as individuals rather than focus on the disability that they have. For example, just because Lily dislikes mashed potatoes and the smell of perfume, it does not mean that all individuals with Autistic Spectrum Condition have the same sensory difficulties.

It is important to take the time to get to know each individual as a person rather than see the Autistic Spectrum Condition first.

Example!

A new teaching assistant at Lily's school has lots of experience caring for individuals with Autistic Spectrum Condition. It is important that the teaching assistant does not think that Lily is just the same as the other children with Autistic Spectrum Condition she has worked with, but that she gets to know all about Lily as a person. The teaching assistant must see Lily first, *not* the Autistic Spectrum Condition.

2.2 How to use a person-centred approach when working with individuals with Autistic Spectrum Condition

As you learned earlier in this chapter, it is very important to see the individual first and not the disability. This is taking a **person-centred approach** to the care and support of individuals. There are many ways that practitioners can take a person-centred approach to supporting people with Autistic Spectrum Condition.

Behavioural characteristics of Autistic Spectrum Condition	Ways to take a person-centred approach
Changes to normal routines cause anxiety and upset	Find ways to keep routines as normal as possible. When routines do have to change, prepare the person in a way that will cause the least anxiety and upset.
Does not like being in places where there are lots of people	Plan to take the person out shopping when shops are quiet and less crowded.
Does not like loud noises	Understand the kind of noises that upset the person with Autistic Spectrum Condition and make sure that, where possible, the noises are removed or the person is taken to another room to enjoy a different activity – for example, during a music activity where drums are being used.
Difficulty communicating and making friends	Practitioners can plan activities for small groups so it is easier for the person with Autistic Spectrum Condition to join in.

Table 14.2 Ways to take a person-centred approach to supporting people with Autistic Spectrum Condition

Important words

Person-centred approach – understanding a person's individual needs and caring for them in the way that suits them best

Assessment task 2.1 2.2

Peter is 41 years old and has Autistic Spectrum Condition. This affects his independence, so he lives in a care home with four other people with Autistic Spectrum Condition. Peter has his own room but shares other areas of the house. The carers understand that the individuals in the house all have different behavioural characteristics and always try to use a person-centred approach to Peter's care.

Complete the table below to show how the carers can best support Peter and manage his behavioural characteristics.

Peter's behavioural characteristics	Ways to take a person-centred approach to Peter's care
Peter does not like to wear clothing with long sleeves.	Where possible, provide Peter with short-sleeved shirts and t-shirts. When Peter needs to go outside in cold weather, provide him with a coat made from a material that least upsets him, and give him time and support to put the coat on.
Peter does not like sitting at the table with other people when eating meals.	
Peter does not like the music that is played during the morning exercise activity.	

Table 14.3 How carers can best support Peter

LO3 The importance of effective communication for individuals with Autistic Spectrum Condition

3.1 3.2 Effective communication that can be used when working with people with Autistic Spectrum Condition

People with Autistic Spectrum Condition very often find it difficult to communicate with other people, and also have difficulty with what other people mean when they are talking. For example, when it is raining hard, someone may say, 'It is throwing it down.' A person with Autistic Spectrum Condition may look to see what someone is throwing.

People with Autistic Spectrum Condition also may find it difficult to understand jokes or funny or sarcastic comments. This means that they may become upset about the things that people around them say.

We know that people with Autistic Spectrum Condition often find communication difficult. Practitioners working in health, social and childcare need to be able to communicate in a way that meets individual needs effectively – they need to use **effective communication**.

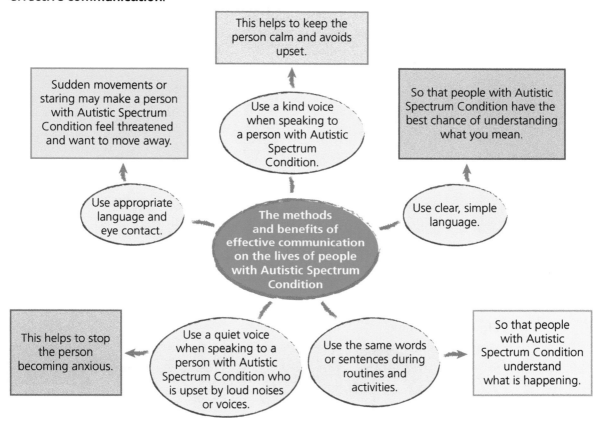

Figure 14.3 The methods and benefits of effective communication on the lives of people with Autistic Spectrum Condition

Important words

Effective communication – giving information in a way that best suits an individual

Assessment task 3.1 3.2 3.3

Describe one way to communicate with Lily and one way to communicate with Peter that meets their individual needs.

3.3 Use of visual communication systems for people with Autistic Spectrum Condition

Many people with Autistic Spectrum Condition can benefit from the use of visual forms of communication, or **visual communication systems**.

Figure 14.4 Eating

Figure 14.5 Getting dressed

Figure 14.6 Going for a walk

Using pictures or photographs to show people with Autistic Spectrum Condition what they will be doing next helps them to know about daily routines when they find spoken language difficult to understand.

Practitioners at Lily's school have put a set of pictures together that help Lily understand her daily school routine. This is known as a 'visual timetable' and the teaching assistant can use this by pointing to different pictures to show Lily what she will be doing next. This also prepares Lily for changes that will be happening during the school day, helps keep her calm and stops her becoming anxious or angry.

Important words

Visual communication systems – form of communication that includes the use of pictures to support communication and understanding

Task

Make a visual timetable for Lily by putting together a set of pictures or drawings to show her what will be happening during the school day.

Write down why you think your visual timetable would help Lily during the school day.

Summary

In this unit, you have learned that:

- 'Autistic Spectrum Condition' is a disability that affects a person's understanding and behaviour and not the way they look
- people with Autistic Spectrum Condition show different behavioural characteristics and often have sensory difficulties that may affect their sense of touch, smell, taste, sight or hearing
- preparation and planning is very important to best support the needs of people with Autistic Spectrum Condition
- using a person-centred approach is important to best care for and support people with Autistic Spectrum Condition because everyone has individual needs
- practitioners must find the best ways to communicate with a person with Autistic Spectrum Condition to help their understanding of the world around them
- different communication methods such as visual pictures or photographs can help people with Autistic Spectrum Condition understand daily routines and when changes are going to happen.

Chapter 15

INTRO OP 1.6 Introduction to physical disability

What you will learn in this unit
You will gain an understanding of:
- the importance of recognising and valuing children, young people and adults with a physical disability
- the main causes of physical disability
- the challenges of living with a physical disability.

LO1 The main causes of physical disability

1.1 Conditions that cause physical disability

There are many reasons why a person may have a physical disability.

Some people are born with physical disability; this type of disability is called *congenital*. An example of congenital disability is spina bifida. This condition is caused when the baby's spinal cord does not properly develop in the womb.

Disability can also be caused by *accidents* which damage the body. Road accidents are the biggest cause of this type of physical disability.

Brain injuries can also cause physical disability. This happens if the part of the brain which controls movement is damaged. Brain injuries like this can sometimes happen during birth but also can happen later in life. Cerebral palsy is an example of a brain injury that happens when the parts of the brain which control movement are starved of oxygen. This can be during birth or because of an illness that stops oxygen getting to the brain.

Illness from viruses and bacteria can cause physical disability by damaging the body systems that control movement. Meningitis can cause the tissues in the fingers and toes to become diseased and die, which sometimes means that affected parts of the body have to be removed to stop the disease spreading.

Some physical disability is *genetic*, which means that one or both parents have passed on a gene that caused disease or disability. An example of a genetic physical disability is muscular dystrophy. This means that a child's muscles get weaker over time and the child stops being able to walk or is not able to move around as well as they used to.

Assessment task 1.1

Complete the table below showing some examples of physical disability. Give a short description of the disability and state whether the disability is congenital/genetic or most likely caused by accident or illness.

Physical disability	Description	Congenital/genetic or caused by accident/illness
Muscular dystrophy	Muscles get weaker over time and movement becomes more difficult	Genetic
Cerebral palsy		Congenital
Spinal cord injury		Accident
Spina bifida		
Amputation		Accident/illness
Arthritis		

Table 15.1 Examples of physical disability

Task

Research on the internet other causes of physical disability.

LO2 The importance of a person-centred approach when working with individuals with a physical disability

2.1 The importance of recognising and valuing individuals with a physical disability

It is very important to see an individual who has physical disability as a person with feelings and needs first, rather than focusing on the disability first.

It is important to value the person first for many reasons. There is a law called the Equality Act 2010, which says that any person with a disability must have the same opportunities as those without a disability. This means that it is against the law for anyone to discriminate against someone with a disability.

It is important to understand what support a person who has a disability might need to live their daily lives as normally as possible. A person with a disability should have the same opportunities in life as people without a disability; this is called 'having equal opportunities'. In order to give people with disability equal opportunities, special equipment or help and support from other people may be needed.

Figure 15.1 A person with a disability should have the same opportunities in life as people without a disability

Equal opportunity does not mean treating everyone the same; it means looking at individual needs and finding ways to give everyone a chance to take part. For example, not everyone with a physical disability requires a wheelchair, so just having wheelchairs available will not suit all people with a disability.

People with a physical disability should be allowed to make as many decisions as they can for themselves so that they feel in control of their own lives. By valuing the person, and not seeing the disability first, the needs of the person can be more easily understood. They will know that their opinions and feelings matter and they may feel more able to make important decisions about what happens to them. This may help them to feel more in control of their own lives.

2.2 Examples of using the person-centred approach when working with individuals with a physical disability

To use the **person-centred approach**, care workers or health professionals should have a good understanding of the needs of the person with a disability. Care workers should take time to find out about the person's opinions, needs, likes and dislikes by asking the right questions and listening carefully to their answers.

The person-centred approach makes sure the person with a disability is listened to and their opinions are valued. It may be that the person with a disability likes to do things in a different way to others and the person-centred approach allows the person to make their own choices. Care workers using the person-centred approach should give people with disability every chance to be able to make choices for themselves.

Often people with a physical disability feel that they struggle to do the things that other people can easily do and this can make them feel very frustrated or upset. The person-centred approach means that care workers need to show they understand the difficulties that the person with a physical disability might have and be able to offer the right choices of support.

Important words

Person-centred approach – understanding a person's individual needs and caring for them in the way that suits them best

Assessment task 2.1 2.2

Make a leaflet for people working in care services that:
- tells them about the person-centred approach
- explains why the person-centred approach should be used when supporting people with a disability.

LO3 How the challenges of living with a physical disability can be addressed

3.1 Factors that have a disabling effect on an individual

There are many factors that can have a disabling effect on an individual.

Environment

The environment can have a disabling effect on a person with a physical disability if care is not taken to look at the changes needed to make it safe and accessible to everyone.

For example, if a group of teenagers decides to go to listen to live music, and one of the teenagers is a wheelchair user but the building does not have wheelchair access, that person will not be able to go with their friends. This would make that person feel left out and not part of the group.

Figure 15.2 A building without wheelchair access

Attitudes and beliefs

Discrimination happens when the attitudes and beliefs towards people with physical disability are not positive. This can happen when others do not see the person with a physical disability as a person, like themselves, with feelings, wishes and opinions.

Sometimes people feel uncomfortable around a person with physical disability. This might not be because they are thinking unkind things, but because they do not understand disability so they do not know how to behave.

Culture

Some cultures are not very understanding of people with physical disability. If a culture does not understand about physical disability, poor attitudes and unkind behaviour towards people with disability are not questioned or challenged. These types of culture do not understand the importance of including people with physical disability in their society; this can make the person with a disability feel that they are not part of normal society.

3.2 Examples of how to challenge discriminatory attitudes

It is important to **challenge discriminatory attitudes** because a person with a physical disability is a person first, with feelings, needs and wishes. If a person with a physical disability feels discriminated against or not fully included in society because of the attitudes of others, this could leave them feeling sad, lonely, depressed and perhaps angry.

When working in health, social care and childcare, it is important to be a good role model and treat people who have a disability with kindness and respect. By treating people with a physical disability respectfully, care workers are showing others who are not so understanding how to behave and the right way to treat people.

If you notice any discriminatory behaviour or feel the attitudes of others are discriminatory, it is important to carefully challenge this, perhaps by asking the person why they have behaved in this way and telling them why it is wrong.

Important words

Challenging discriminatory attitudes – this means telling people who treat individuals with disability in an unkind way that they are wrong and must change their attitude or behaviour

3.3 The effects that having a physical disability can have on an individual's day-to-day life

Having a physical disability can have lots of effects on a person's day-to-day life, and these can include:

◆ difficulty getting into and around buildings safely and easily
◆ having to deal with other people's discriminatory attitudes
◆ tiredness, because of the extra physical effort needed to move around
◆ problems using equipment such as pens, mobile phones, kitchen utensils, machinery and computers
◆ difficulties in travelling during busy times, for example, busy pavements, crowded trains or buses
◆ the side-effects of some medicines, such as tiredness or feeling unwell.

Figure 15.3 Difficulty travelling during busy times

Figure 15.4 Problems using equipment such as pens

Assessment task 3.1 3.2 3.3

Make a poster for school children to:
◆ explain how culture, environment, attitudes and beliefs can have a disabling effect on an individual
◆ give examples of how to challenge discriminatory attitudes
◆ explain the effects that having a physical disability can have on an individual's day-to-day life.

3.4 How individuals can be in control of their care needs

People with a disability may feel that they do not have the same choices or control over their lives as other people. For people with a disability to have equal opportunities, it is important to allow them to make choices about what happens to them. Being at the centre of making decisions about their own care allows a person to feel in control. Ways this can happen are shown in Figure 15.5.

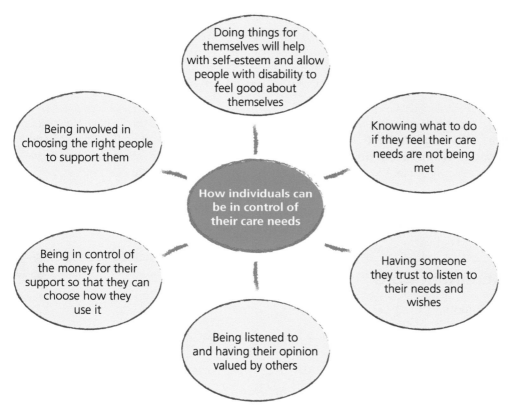

Figure 15.5 How individuals can be in control of their care needs

3.5 The importance of promoting independence for individuals with physical disability

> **Important words** !
>
> **Promoting independence** – encouraging someone to find ways to do things for themselves

Everyone likes to be independent and in control of their own lives. This is exactly the same for a person with a physical disability.

Having support to live independently is very important for a person with a physical disability. One reason is that when a person is independent and can meet their own care needs, they may have more self-respect and there is less opportunity for abuse to take place.

By not always having to ask others for help, people with a physical disability may feel more confident about managing their disability.

By being independent, a person with a physical disability can perform day-to-day tasks in the way they want to do them and when they want to do them. This will make them feel in control.

3.6 Ways to promote the inclusion of individuals with physical disability in society

There are many ways to promote **inclusion** of people with physical disability in society. Pictures in magazines and books, and images on the internet and on the television now show positive images of people with physical disability. When we see good images, we are more likely to see the positive side rather than the negative side of something.

For example, when we see pictures of people with a physical disability taking part in sports activities such as the Paralympics, or taking on difficult physical challenges such as climbing mountains, we stop thinking that people with a physical disability cannot be fit and active.

Important word

Inclusion – being part of something, and making sure everyone is included in a fair and equal way

Figure 15.6 A sprint runner with a prosthetic leg

Since the Equality Act 2010, shops and public places such as cinemas, sports centres and cafes must do everything possible to make these places safe and easy for people with physical disability to move around independently.

Figure 15.7 Wheelchair access to the pool

Assessment task 3.4 3.5 3.6

Write a page on a website for young people about physical disability. On the page, include:

◆ examples of how people with physical disability can be in control of their care needs
◆ why it is important to promote independence for individuals with physical disability
◆ ways to promote the inclusion of individuals with physical disability in society.

Summary

In this unit, you have learned that:

◆ it is important to recognise and value children, young people and adults with a physical disability
◆ there are many causes of physical disability
◆ there are many challenges of living with a physical disability
◆ discriminatory attitudes must always be challenged
◆ it is important to promote inclusion and independence for individuals with physical disability.

Chapter 16

What you will learn in this unit

You will gain an understanding of:

◆ the importance of recognising and valuing individuals with mental health problems

◆ how to use a person-centred approach when working with individuals with mental health problems

◆ types and causes of mental health problems

◆ the importance of effective communication with individuals who have mental health problems.

LO1 The main factors that can cause mental health problems

1.1 Factors that affect mental health

There are many factors that can affect **mental health**:

◆ *Emotional factors* – this is when an individual feels very emotional, perhaps because something has gone wrong in their lives, they have had a bad experience or they have suffered the loss of someone close to them.

◆ *Social factors* – this is when an individual feels that they have no friends or they feel left out or all alone. This could be caused by being unemployed or not having enough money to join in any social activities.

◆ *Psychological factors* – this is when someone has a certain fear, is coping with trauma such as abuse or may have a phobia; for example, being afraid to leave the house.

◆ *Biochemical factors* – this is when chemicals in the brain change how a person thinks and feels.

◆ *Genetic factors* – this is about the information in our cells (DNA) that we get from our parents, which affects the way we look, think and behave.

◆ *Physical factors* – this is when an individual has a disability that makes them feel different, or they are worried about how they look and how others might see them.

Important words

Mental health – how a person's thinking makes them feel

Figure 16.1 Feeling left out may affect an individual's mental health

1.2 Examples of different mental health problems

There is a wide range of mental health problems that can affect an individual, and these can include:

◆ *Depression* – this can affect an individual's mood; they may feel sad or lonely. They may not feel good about themselves. Sometimes an individual with depression may not want to carry out their usual routine. For example, they will not want to get out of bed in the morning, or will not want to spend time with their friends.

◆ *Anxiety* – this can make an individual look or feel scared. Sometimes individuals may have panic attacks, feel very nervous or not be able to sleep well.

◆ *Self-harm* – this is when an individual cuts, hurts or injures themselves on purpose.

◆ *Eating disorders* – this sometimes includes overeating, cutting out food groups or not eating enough food to stay healthy.

◆ *Stress* – this can involve feeling worried, anxious or tense. An individual who is stressed may not be able to sleep well, and their eating habits might change, for example, overeating or not feeling able to eat.

- *Bipolar disorder* – a person's moods change between high and low; for example, sometimes being over-excited or at other times feeling very sad and unhappy. Sometimes an individual with bipolar disorder will behave normally and at other times their behaviour will seem very strange.
- *Schizophrenia* – when an individual imagines that characters or voices that are in their head are real. They may think the characters are talking to them and telling them to do things. Sometimes an individual with schizophrenia will think the voices and characters in their head can harm them.

Assessment task 1.1 1.2

Write an information leaflet for somebody new to working with people with mental health problems. In the leaflet:
- give information about factors that affect mental health
- write down four examples of mental health problems.

LO2 The importance of a person-centred approach when working with individuals with mental health problems

2.1 Why it is important to recognise and value an individual with mental health problems as a person first

It is very important to see an individual with mental health problems as a person with feelings and wishes first, rather than focusing on the mental health problems.

This is important for many reasons. One reason is that there is a law called the **Mental Capacity Act**, which says that adults with mental health problems should be allowed to make as many decisions as they can for themselves.

A person with mental health problems may feel out of control or feel that no one is listening to them, so it is important that they feel both listened to and in control of what is happening to them.

By valuing the person first, not the mental health problem, the needs of the person can be more easily understood.

When supporting a person with mental health problems, it is important to find out about the person's needs, wishes, likes and dislikes. Everyone has different ideas about what they need and want, and these wishes should be taken into account when looking for the best ways to support the person.

Important words

Mental Capacity Act – a law made to protect people who are experiencing poor mental health

Figure 16.2 Supporting a person with mental health problems

2.2 How to use a person-centred approach when working with individuals with mental health problems

In using a **person-centred approach**, care workers or health professionals should have a good understanding of the way the person with mental health problems feels and behaves. Care workers should also find out about the person's wishes, needs, likes and dislikes by asking the right questions and listening carefully to their answers.

Care workers may need to get information about the person with mental health problems from other places, such as personal information records or by talking to family and friends. Confidentiality rules should always be followed to keep the individual and the care workers safe.

Often people with mental health problems feel very worried or anxious about what is happening to them. The person-centred approach means that care workers need to understand these fears and worries, and offer the right support.

> ## Important words
>
> **Person-centred approach** – understanding a person's individual needs and caring for them in the way that suits them best

Assessment task 2.1 2.2

Add to your leaflet:
- Explain why it is important to recognise and value individuals with mental health problems as people first.
- Give examples of how to use a person-centred approach when working with individuals with mental health problems.

LO3 The importance of effective communication with individuals who have mental health problems

3.1 The benefits of effective communication on the lives of individuals with mental health problems

It is very important to communicate well with people who have mental health problems. This could make the difference between a person feeling supported and listened to or feeling isolated and alone.

> **Important words** ❗
>
> **Effective communication** – giving information in a way that best suits an individual

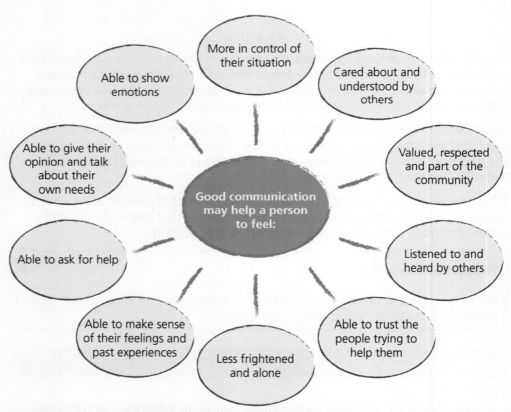

Figure 16.3 The benefits of **effective communication** on the lives of individuals with mental health problems

3.2 The importance of using active listening skills with individuals who have mental health problems

Active listening is important as this is the main way to find out information about a person with mental health problems. Active listening happens when the professional listens very carefully to what is being said and is not distracted by other things around them. It should take place in a quiet space with no background noise, away from other people.

Active listening helps by giving a person time to tell you about how they feel, what they need and what is happening to them in their lives.

Active listening can be difficult as we may not always listen carefully to what others are saying because we are thinking about our own opinions or what we need to say next. When we listen actively, we need to focus on what is being said and also make sure that we have good eye contact and positive body language. This shows the person we are listening carefully and are interested in what they are saying.

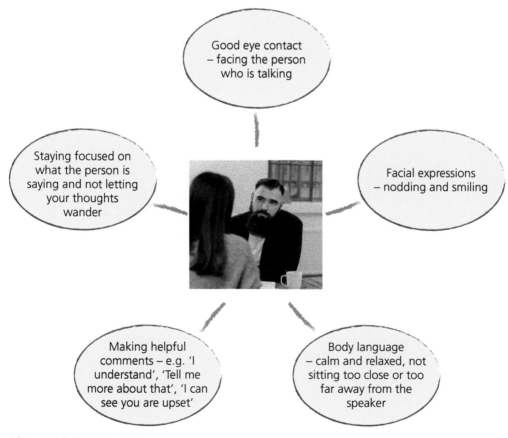

Figure 16.4 Active listening

Assessment task 3.1 3.2

In your leaflet, include information about:
- ◆ the benefits of effective communication
- ◆ the importance of using active listening.

Summary

In this unit, you have learned that:

- ◆ it is important to recognise and value individuals with mental health problems
- ◆ a person-centred approach should be used when working with individuals with mental health problems
- ◆ there are different types and causes of mental health problems
- ◆ it is important to use effective communication with individuals who have mental health problems.

Chapter 17

What you will learn in this unit

You will gain an understanding of:

◆ why it is important to recognise and value an individual with dementia as a person first
◆ the person-centred approach
◆ what is meant by dementia and the main causes of dementia
◆ the effects of dementia on families and carers
◆ the benefits of effective communication in the lives of individuals with dementia
◆ how memory loss affects the use of spoken language in an individual with dementia
◆ techniques that can be used to facilitate communication with an individual with dementia.

LO1 The main causes and effects of dementia

1.1 What is meant by 'dementia'?

Dementia is a word used to describe a slow loss of memory and thinking skills. This happens because cells in the brain stop working properly. The parts of the brain that are usually affected are the parts that control how we think, remember and communicate.

Important word

Dementia – a disease that damages the brain, causing a person to forget things, be unable to think clearly or lose the ability to speak

1.2 Examples of the causes of dementia

There is still a lot of information for doctors and scientists to discover and learn about dementia, but there are four main causes.

Alzheimer's disease	Scientists have found that Alzheimer's disease happens when *proteins build up in the brain* and they attach themselves to cells. When this happens, the part of the brain that makes new memories stops working first.
Vascular dementia	Vascular dementia is caused when the *blood flow to the brain is not good enough.* Blood carries oxygen to the brain and, without it, brain cells can die. This causes the brain to stop working properly and affects memory, language and attention span.
Fronto-temporal dementia	This is a disease that causes some *parts of the brain to shrink* and get smaller. This usually affects the front of the brain, which controls behaviour, emotions, decision making and language.
Dementia with Lewy bodies	Lewy bodies dementia is similar to Alzheimer's because proteins build up in cells in the brain. *Nerve cells are affected by Lewy bodies* in parts of the brain that control thinking, memory and movement.

Table 17.1 Examples of the causes of dementia

1.3 The effects of dementia on individuals, families and carers

It can be very stressful when a person starts to experience signs of dementia, such as forgetting where they have put things or what they have just said. The person may become very worried about losing their memory, and feel stressed about how they and their families will cope with this disease.

Having a family member with dementia can have an effect on all members of the family. Some of the most common feelings family members may have are *guilt, grief, sadness* and *anger.*

Some family members may feel embarrassed by the strange things the person with dementia says or does, and then they feel guilty for *feeling embarrassed* by the person who they love and care about.

People with dementia can sometimes become difficult to manage or they may become angry and aggressive. If this causes a family member to *lose patience* with the person who has dementia, they may feel very guilty for shouting or getting cross.

If someone in a family develops dementia, other family members may feel they have lost the person they knew and almost *feel grief* similar to that felt when someone close to them dies. The feeling of grief is for the *loss of the future* that they might have shared with the person who now has dementia.

Sometimes family members may *feel worried* about how they will cope in the future, worrying about having to put their loved one in a care home, or they may worry about children in the family seeing the odd behaviour of the family member who has dementia.

It may be that some family members *feel trapped* in their own homes, as they are not able to leave the person with dementia alone at home, so they *stop going out*. The carer may then *lose contact with friends* and begin to *feel lonely*, and perhaps *angry* that this is happening.

Figure 17.1 The feeling of grief

Assessment task 1.1 1.2 1.3

Produce an information leaflet for families explaining:
◆ what is meant by dementia
◆ the causes of dementia.

Include a spider diagram or list of the effects of dementia on families and carers.

LO2 The importance of a person-centred approach when working with individuals with dementia

2.1 The importance of recognising and valuing an individual with dementia as a person first

The **person-centred approach** sees the person with dementia as an important individual who has their own interests, opinions, likes and dislikes. Not every person with dementia will need the same type of care and the person-centred approach puts the needs of the individual first.

Health care workers using the person-centred approach find out about the person's individual needs and interests when deciding how to care for them. Individuals should always be treated with dignity and respect.

Figure 17.2 The person-centred approach puts the needs of the individual first

Important words

Person-centred approach – understanding a person's individual needs and caring for them in the way that suits them best

2.2 How to use a person-centred approach when working with individuals with dementia

This staff member should have a clear idea of the life history, routines and interests of a person with dementia. Although an individual with dementia may not be able to take care of themselves safely, it is important to give them safe choices, such as what clothes they would like to wear, if they would like to take part in activities or where they like to sit in a room.

To use the person-centred approach, care workers need to learn about the life history of a person with dementia so that they can talk to the person about their earlier life and provide activities that may bring back happy memories of times or places they enjoyed when they were younger. If the person with dementia can do particular things for themselves, they should be encouraged to continue to do so as it will help to keep them active.

Often people with dementia feel worried or anxious about what is happening to them. The person-centred approach also means that workers need to understand the fears and worries that the person with dementia might have and give them the right support.

Assessment task 2.1 2.2

Make a poster for a doctors' surgery giving information about:
◆ why it is important to recognise and value an individual with dementia as a person first
◆ how to use a person-centred approach when working with individuals with dementia.

LO3 The importance of effective communication for individuals with dementia

3.1 The benefits of effective communication on the lives of individuals with dementia

There are many benefits of effective communication on the lives of individuals with dementia, as shown in Figure 17.3.

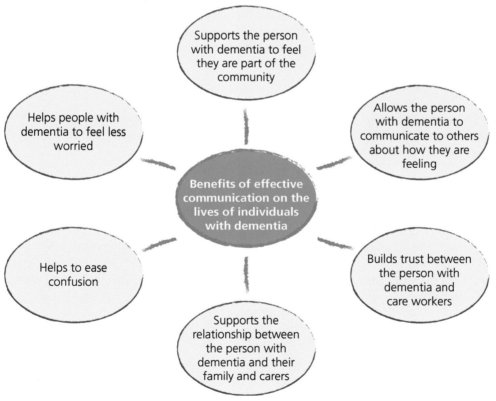

Figure 17.3 The benefits of effective communication on the lives of individuals with dementia

3.2 How memory loss affects the use of spoken language in an individual with dementia

Dementia is an illness which will always get worse over time. The illness slows down the person's ability to think clearly and understand information. This means that a person will find it difficult or impossible to remember things such as people's names – even very close family members' names; they will forget dates and places they have been.

Dementia will slowly stop the person communicating with other people because they forget the meaning of words needed to make conversation.

3.3 Examples of techniques that can be used to support communication with an individual with dementia

It is important to keep a person with dementia involved in making conversation for as long as it is possible to do so. Ways to encourage communication include the following:
- Use good eye contact and smiling to make the person feel comfortable.
- Active listening – try not to interrupt the person when they are speaking.
- Speak clearly and slowly so the person has time to think about what is being said.
- Be patient and calm, and give the person time to find the words they want to use.
- Use a friendly tone of voice to reassure the person.
- Hold or pat the person's hand to help them feel safe and relaxed.
- Use pictures or items from the person's past to help bring back happy memories.

Task

Go to **www.nhs.uk/Conditions/dementia-guide/Pages/dementia-and-communication.aspx** and read about the many other ways to communicate with people with dementia.

Assessment task 3.1 3.2 3.3

Make lists to show:
- the benefits of effective communication on the lives of individuals with dementia
- how memory loss affects the use of spoken language in an individual with dementia
- ways to communicate with an individual with dementia.

Summary

In this unit, you have learned:

- that dementia is a disease that affects a person's memory and communication
- why it is important to recognise and value an individual with dementia as a person first
- how to use the person-centred approach
- the meaning of dementia and the main causes of dementia
- how dementia can affect families and carers
- the benefits of effective communication on the lives of individuals with dementia
- that memory loss affects the use of spoken language in an individual with dementia
- ways to communicate with an individual with dementia.

Chapter 18

INTRO OP 1.11 Introduction to the physical care needs of babies and young children

What you will learn in this unit

You will gain an understanding of:

◆ the care needs of babies and young children
◆ how to treat babies and young children with respect and sensitivity
◆ how to engage babies and young children during physical care routines
◆ the principles of toilet training
◆ how to provide a safe and hygienic environment for babies and young children
◆ how to safely supervise babies and young children
◆ what to do to support the well-being of babies and young children
◆ the nutritional needs and allergies of young children.

LO1 The physical care needs of babies and young children

1.1 Care needs for babies and young children

Skin

A baby's skin can easily be damaged so it is important to use only gentle soaps and shampoos. Baby bath products are made without any harsh chemicals so are just right for cleaning a baby's or young child's skin. You should never rub a baby's skin but gently wipe with a clean, wet soft cloth.

You do not need to bath a very young baby every day, but it is important to keep their skin clean and this can be done by top and tailing.

How to top and tail a young baby

◆ Gently undress the baby, but leave their nappy on.
◆ Wrap the baby in a soft, dry towel.
◆ Place the baby on the floor on a changing mat.
◆ Using clean, warm water, dip a clean piece of cotton wool in the water and gently clean the baby's face, taking care around the eyes, nose and ears. Use a different piece of cotton wool for each eye.
◆ Wash the baby's hands and neck area and gently dry them with the towel.
◆ Unwrap the towel from the baby and take off their nappy. Wash the nappy area, taking care to clean the folds and creases of the skin. Gently dry well with the towel and put on a clean nappy.
◆ Dress the baby.
◆ Talk to the baby about what you are doing, smile and give them eye contact – this will help them to relax.

Safety rules when caring for skin ⚠

- *Never* leave the baby alone near water.
- *Always* place the baby on the floor on a mat so that they cannot roll off a high surface and get hurt.
- *Never* poke cotton buds into the baby's ears or nose as this can cause damage.

Bath time

It is important to make bath time a relaxing, enjoyable time for babies and young children. Young children may enjoy playing with bath toys or helping to wash their own hair. Bath time is a good time to clean a child's teeth.

Figure 18.1 Bath time should be relaxing and enjoyable

Bathing a young baby

- Choose a good time to bath a baby, not straight after a feed or when they are hungry or very tired.
- Get everything you need together, including a bath of warm water, a soft cloth, cotton wool, a clean, dry towel, bath shampoo and baby bath liquid, a clean nappy and clean clothes.
- Check the temperature of the bath water.
- Clean the baby's face first (read how to do this in the top and tailing section).
- Wrap the baby up using the towel and hold them over the bath to gently wash their hair using a gentle baby shampoo; rinse with the warm water.
- Gently dry the baby's hair with the towel.
- Take off the baby's nappy and wipe away any mess.
- Place the baby in the bath, using one arm to support their head and shoulders.
- Gently splash the warm water over the child using a clean cloth, taking care to wash in the creases and folds of skin around the arms and legs.

Figure 18.2 How to support a baby in the bath

Bathing a child

Once a child can sit comfortably and safely without the support of an adult, bath time is a much simpler routine. Remember a child will move around much quicker than a young baby so it is important to watch them carefully.

Always put cold water into the bath first and add hot water until the water is warm enough. This way of filling the bath should always be used because children can quickly climb into the bath before the bath is ready and hot water could seriously burn their skin.

- Get everything ready, including a bath of warm water, soap, hair shampoo, face cloth, clean towels, bath toys, clean clothes and a clean nappy (if the child wears nappies).
- Undress the child and sit them in the bath.
- Talk to the child about what is happening and *do not* leave the child alone in the bath – not even for a few seconds.
- Wash the child, taking care when cleaning their face.
- Wash hair, using a gentle shampoo – the child may like to help. Rinse hair with clean water – using a shower or jug is a good idea.
- Let the child play for a while, but don't let them get too cold.
- Gently lift the child out of the water – take the plug out so that the water drains away.
- Carefully dry the child and dress them. Dry their hair as needed.

Check out this NHS web page for a demonstration of bathing a baby:
www.nhs.uk/Conditions/pregnancy-and-baby/Pages/washing-your-baby.aspx#close

Safety rules when bathing 3.1 3.2

- *Always* **supervise** the child around water and never leave them alone in water – not even for a few seconds.
- *Always* put the cold water into the bath first so that if the child climbs into the bath before you are ready, the water will not burn the child.
- *Always* check the temperature, either with your elbow or with a bath thermometer so that the water is not too hot or too cold (move the water around the bath to check there are no hot areas).
- Make sure the bath water is not too deep.
- *Never* take any electrical items such as heaters or music players into the bathroom.

Important word

Supervise – to watch a baby or child to make sure they are staying safe

Hair

A young baby does not need to have their hair washed every day. When a baby is being weaned or learning to eat food by themselves, they often get very messy and food may get into their hair, so it is important to wash it more regularly.

It is best to wash a baby or child's hair during bath time, using a mild shampoo. It is important to rinse hair well to get rid of all of the shampoo. Take care with the temperature of the water and always supervise children when they are in the bath.

Hair should be carefully brushed with a soft bristled brush.

Figure 18.3 Some equipment for bathing a baby

Head lice

If a child comes into contact with other children – for example, brothers and sisters or friends at nursery – it is important to check their hair regularly for head lice as this is a common problem.

Head lice are tiny, wingless insects that attach themselves to the scalp.

It is very difficult to see head lice, and using a fine-toothed lice comb is the best way to find them. Head lice can be treated using special lotions or by wet combing using conditioner and a lice comb. Wet combing done every two days for about 14 days should get rid of the lice.

Further information can be found on the following NHS web page:
www.nhs.uk/conditions/Head-lice/Pages/Introduction.aspx

Teeth

A young child will get 20 first teeth, which are called milk teeth, and the first tooth cuts through the gums at around six months of age. Some babies will cut their teeth without many problems, but other babies have signs of teething such as shown in Figure 18.4.

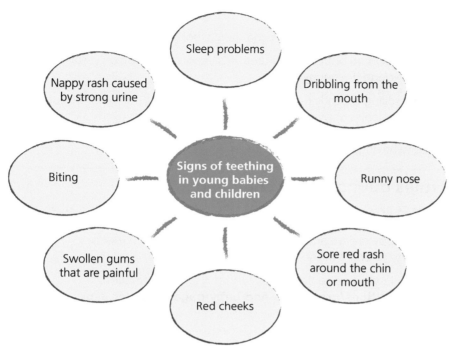

Figure 18.4 Signs of teething in young babies and children

Care of teeth

◆ It is important to start cleaning a young child's teeth, twice a day, as soon as the first tooth cuts through the gums.

◆ Teeth cleaning should happen every morning and every evening to keep teeth clean and healthy (bath time is a good time to brush a child's teeth).

◆ Start by doing all the brushing for the young child but, as the child gets older, let them have a go first. By the time the child is about eight years old, they should be able to brush their own teeth properly. Use a mirror so that the child can see what they are doing.

◆ Use a soft toothbrush and mild fluoride toothpaste when brushing children's teeth.

◆ Brush teeth for two minutes (using an egg timer set for two minutes is a good idea).

◆ Visit the dentist as soon as the first teeth come through and then follow advice about how often to take the child to see the dentist.

◆ A low-sugar diet will help to keep teeth healthy and strong.

Safety rules when caring for hair and teeth

• *Always* supervise children around water.

• *Never* let a child run around with a toothbrush in their mouth as they could fall and injure their mouth or throat.

• *Do not* let children eat toothpaste as too much fluoride can be harmful to young children.

Nappy area

Always wash your hands before and after changing a baby's nappy.

When caring for a newborn baby's nappy area, it is important to use only warm water and cotton wool to clean the nappy area.

Make sure that all soiling is gently removed and take care to get the creases clean and dry before putting a clean nappy on the baby. Some babies with sensitive skin need to have a very regular nappy changing routine because they can easily get sore skin in the nappy area due to having a wet nappy.

Safety rules during nappy changing 3.1 3.2

- *Never* leave or turn your back on a baby who is lying on a changing table as they could easily roll off and be seriously injured.
- *Never* leave nappy cream and lotions in a place a baby can reach.
- *Always* put dirty nappies in the outside bin.

The following NHS web page has some further useful information:
www.nhs.uk/Conditions/pregnancy-and-baby/pages/nappies.aspx

Task

You are caring for a baby aged six months. Make a list of all the safety rules when nappy changing and bathing the child.

Assessment task 1.1

Using the information you have learned, complete the table below by identifying the physical care needs of babies and young children.

Care of babies and young children	Identify the care needs for each area
Skin	
Hair	
Teeth	
Nappy area	

Table 18.1 The care needs of babies and young children

LO2 How to support physical care routines for babies and young children

2.1 How to treat babies and young children with respect and sensitivity during physical care routines

It is important to always treat babies and young children with respect and sensitivity during **physical care routines**. Treating children with respect and sensitivity will help them to become confident and feel good about themselves.

Know what the child likes and does not like and always act on this information.

For example, some young children enjoy having a bath with bubbles; others do not like, bubbles.

Try and encourage the child to become more independent as they get older.

For example, let the child have a go at brushing their own teeth, and then finish it for them to make sure the teeth are clean.

Always think about the young child's privacy.

For example, change nappies and allow children to use the potty in a place where others are not able to watchthem.

Praise the child when they have done something well and try to ignore any mistakes.

For example, never make fun of the child or make them feel bad about themselves by calling the child silly or laughing at them when they have a toilet accident. Never make faces or comment on any bad smells the child may make as this might make the child feel like they have done something wrong.

Ways to show babies and young children respect and sensitivity during physical care routines

Tell the child what you are going to do so that they know what to expect.

For example, during bath time you could say, 'Now it's time to put the shampoo on your hair', so that the child knows what is happening.

Speak kindly to the baby or young child and never shout or get angry.

For example, some babies wriggle a lot during nappy changing, so talk to them about what you are doing and give good eye contact, or perhaps give them a toy to distract them. Never get cross with an unhappy child as this will only upset them more.

Always carry out physical care routines gently.

For example, wipe young children's noses carefully so that you do not pinch too hard and hurt them.

Think carefully about the age and needs of the child.

For example, a baby should be held closely when having a milk feed, but a toddler should be seated safely in a high chair and then, when old enough, moved into an adult-sized chair to eat their meals.

Figure 18.5 Ways to show babies and young children respect and sensitivity during physical care routines

Important words

Physical care routines – a baby's or child's day-to-day care needs (skin, hair, teeth, nappy area)

Assessment task 2.1

Make a poster for a health centre showing ways to treat babies and young children with respect and sensitivity during physical care routines.

2.2 Ways of engaging with babies and young children during physical care routines that make the experience enjoyable

◆ Talk or sing to a young child during care routines. For example, sing to a baby or young child when changing their nappy.
◆ Speak gently and soothingly. For example, when cleaning a child's sore skin, say gently, 'All finished now'.
◆ Give the baby or young child eye contact and a smile. For example, look and smile at a baby when feeding them.
◆ Know the baby's or young child's likes. For example, know how a baby likes to be held when being given a milk feed.
◆ Ask if it is OK to do something. For example, asking a young child, 'Can I wipe your nose for you?'
◆ Encourage the child to have a go. For example, encourage them to wash their own face.
◆ Join in with the child so it becomes a more enjoyable experience. For example, clean your teeth at the same time as the child cleans theirs.

Assessment task 2.2

List ways to make physical care routines enjoyable for a baby or young child.

2.3 Principles of toilet training

Becoming toilet trained is an important time for a young child and should not be rushed or started before the child is ready.

All young children are very different and it is not always easy to decide when it is the right time to begin toilet training. Most young children will be ready to start toilet training around the age of two years and will feel more comfortable using a potty rather than a normal sized toilet, which may seem very large to a young child.

Signs that a young child is ready to use a potty

A young child should never be forced to use the potty before they are ready. Young children will only be able to use a potty correctly when their bladder and bowel have properly developed. Some signs that a child may be ready to start potty training are shown in Figure 18.6.

Figure 18.6 Some signs that a child may be ready to start potty training

How to start potty training

◆ Leave a potty out somewhere the child can see it and where they can get to it quickly.
◆ It might help to have another potty beside the main toilet so that the child understands toileting routines.
◆ If the child has a dirty nappy at around the same time every day, take their nappy off and have the potty in easy reach.
◆ If the child is upset about sitting on a potty, just put the nappy back on and wait a few more weeks before trying again. Never force a child to sit on a potty as this will upset them and will not help them to become toilet trained.
◆ If the child lets you know they need to wee, offer them the potty. If the child does not make it on to the potty in time or has an accident, wipe up the spill quickly and do not make a big fuss because if the child thinks you are annoyed with them, they may not want to try again.
◆ The child will feel very pleased with themselves when they use the potty correctly. It is important to praise them by telling them they have done well.
◆ Always wash the contents of the potty down the toilet straight away and clean the potty ready to use again.

Figure 18.7 A potty in an easily accessible place

Figure 18.8 A potty beside the main toilet

LO3 How to support safe and protective environments for babies and young children

3.1 3.2 Providing a safe and hygienic environment for babies and young children

Assessment task 3.1 3.2

Using the 'safety rules' earlier in this chapter (page 174), write a checklist for new parents, listing safety rules to follow when changing a baby's nappy.

Important words

Safe and hygienic environment – keeping the space around the baby or child clean and making sure they are safe from harm

3.3 What to do if you are concerned about the well-being of babies and young children

When someone is worried about the well-being of babies and young children, there are important steps to take to help the child. Remember **confidentiality**, which means that the concerns are not talked about to anyone apart from the setting supervisor, police or professionals from support organisations.

Firstly, if you see anything that concerns you, it is important to write down the facts; this will include the times, dates and what it is you have seen or heard. Then, pass this information to your supervisor if you work in a setting, or the child's health care professional, such as a health visitor, doctor or social worker. This information is confidential – it must not be discussed or shared with anyone other than the professionals dealing with the situation.

Important word

Confidentiality – only sharing information with people who need to know or can offer help

Assessment task 3.3

Discuss in groups and make notes about why it is important to maintain confidentiality when there are concerns about the well-being of a child. Write down what might happen if you do not maintain confidentiality about a baby or young child.

LO4 The nutritional needs of babies and young children

4.1 4.2 The nutritional needs of babies and young children

(See Chapter 9, Unit PWCS 07 on pages 87–95 for supporting material.)

The **Department of Health** recommends that, where possible, new mothers breastfeed their babies for the first six months of a baby's life. This is because breast milk contains exactly the right amount of calories needed for energy and the right amount of nutrients to help the baby to develop and grow. Breast milk also contains antibodies from the mother, which help to protect the baby from illness and disease.

Scientists who have researched breast milk say that babies who are breastfed do not have as many upset tummies or infections as bottle-fed babies because of the antibodies in breast milk.

Although breastfeeding is the best nutrition for a young baby, some mothers choose to bottle-feed their babies. Babies who are bottle-fed will have formula milk, which has nutrients which are as close to breast milk as possible.

Important words

Nutritional needs – the food a baby or child needs to grow and stay healthy

Department of Health – a government department that is concerned with the health of the UK's citizens

Weaning

When a baby gets to around six months of age, milk alone no longer provides all the **nutritional needs** for healthy growth and development, so the baby will need to be weaned on to solid foods.

Weaning begins by offering the baby small teaspoons of baby rice mixed with their usual milk and, over time, a wider range of foods are added to the diet.

To begin with, the weaning foods need to be very smooth and easy to swallow, but slowly the food can become more lumpy. By the time the baby is a toddler, they will have teeth, and be able to chew and enjoy finger foods such as toast and carrot sticks. By the time the child is around three years of age, they usually enjoy most of the same foods that adults eat.

The nutrients needed by babies and young children are shown in Figure 18.9.

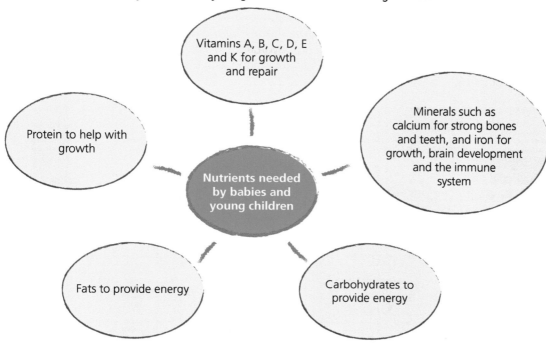

Figure 18.9 Nutrients needed by babies and young children

Which foods contain nutrients?

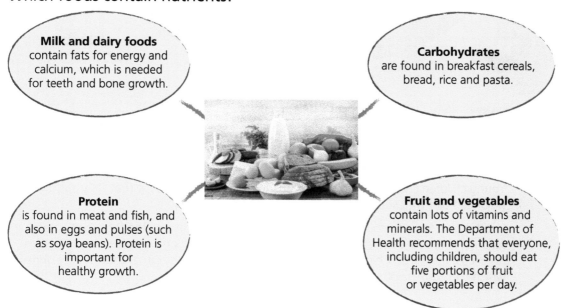

Figure 18.10 Which foods contain nutrients?

4.3 Healthy balanced meals for young children

The Eatwell Guide, shown in Figure 18.11, shows how much of each food type is needed for a healthy diet. The picture shows that the largest part of the diet should come from fruit, vegetables and carbohydrates, such as potatoes and pasta. Milk and dairy products should be eaten every day, along with foods high in protein, such as fish or meat.

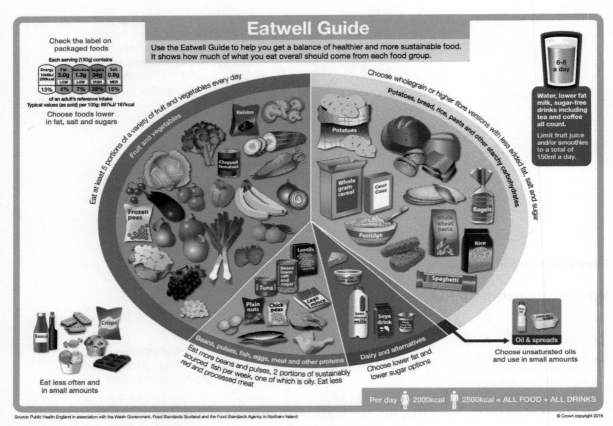

Figure 18.11 The Eatwell Guide

Source: **www.nhs.uk/Livewell/Goodfood/Pages/eatwell-plate.aspx**

Young children can sometimes be fussy eaters, but it is important that they eat a well-balanced diet that supports healthy growth and development.

Food that is given to children should be healthy and nutritious. Bad food that is very high in fat and/or sugar, such as sweets and crisps, should only be given to children as an occasional treat. Children should be offered milk or water rather than sugary drinks, which can cause tooth decay.

Looking at the Eatwell Guide to get the information about which types of foods are needed in a balanced diet, plan a breakfast, lunch and dinner for a young child. Make sure they will get all the nutrients they require for healthy growth and development.

4.4 Nutritional allergies

Some babies and young children become ill when they eat certain foods. These are called **nutritional allergies**. A mild allergy to a food might cause a young child to have a rash, runny nose, tummy pain or diarrhoea. A doctor can test a child for allergies, and the best way to care for a baby or child with a mild allergy is to try and avoid giving the food that causes the problems.

Only a few babies and children have very serious nutritional allergies which cause them to be dangerously ill if they eat certain foods. Eating foods that they are seriously allergic to can cause babies and young children to wheeze or cough, their mouths and tongues can swell so that it is difficult to breathe and they may collapse or go into shock, which can be life-threatening.

Babies and children who have a serious allergy to foods will usually have medication from the doctor or hospital that they can be given if needed. The child should then be taken straight to hospital for treatment.

Important words

Nutritional allergies – when a baby or child becomes ill from eating or touching a certain food

Foods that may cause allergy are shown in Figure 18.12.

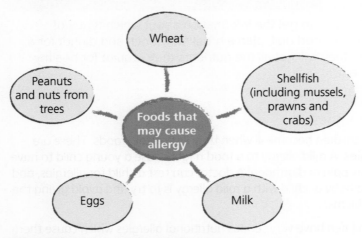

Figure 18.12 Foods that may cause allergy

Assessment task 4.4

Research about nutritional allergies on the internet and:
◆ make a list of three common food allergies in children
◆ describe three signs that show a child may have a food allergy.

Summary

In this unit, you have learned that:
◆ babies and young children have a range of physical care needs
◆ babies and young children should always be treated with respect and sensitivity
◆ physical care routines can be made more enjoyable when the adult engages with the baby or young child
◆ following the principles of toilet training is important
◆ a safe and hygienic environment is very important when caring for babies and young children
◆ babies and young children need constant supervision to keep them safe
◆ there are steps to follow when there is a concern about the well-being of a baby or young child
◆ young children have nutritional needs that can be met through having a balanced diet
◆ it is important to know which foods to avoid when feeding babies and young children.

Chapter 19

Introduction to the development of children and young people through play

What you will learn in this unit

You will gain an understanding of:

- how play supports children and young people's development and well-being
- the difference between adult-led play and child-centred play
- how environments can support inclusive and stimulating play
- activities that support inclusive and stimulating play.

LO1 The importance of play for children's and young people's development and well-being

1.1 How play supports children's and young people's development and well-being

Play is a very important part of children's learning and development. It is through play that children use their senses and, while having fun, they can be creative and also learn about the world around them.

When children and young people play, they are developing new skills and practising skills they have already learned. When children and young people play together, they are learning to socialise and practise team work.

When playing happily with others, children and young people will feel accepted in the group, which will support their emotional well-being. Being outdoors and having exercise while playing will support physical well-being.

Important word

Well-being – an individual's good physical and mental health

When playing outdoors, children and young people are able to learn about risk and challenge. This is when they have to decide for themselves if something is safe to do – for example, jumping off a climbing frame. If the child falls when they land on the ground, they will learn that they have climbed too high to jump safely, but if they land safely, they will know that they have good physical skills and will feel proud of themselves.

Figure 19.1 Children playing outdoors

1.2 The difference between adult-led play and child-centred play

Child-centred play is when the child makes choices about what activities they join in with or what toys they play with. The child makes up the rules and decides how to play and how long to play. During child-centred play, the child is in control and adults will only get involved if the child is not playing safely.

Important words

Child-centred play – play that is started and led by children themselves

Adult-led play – play activities that are planned and run by adults

Figure 19.2 Child-centred play

Adult-led play is when the adult plans the activities and the adult provides the equipment that they would like the child to use. The adult will have a good idea of what the child should be doing or learning and will support the child during play.

Figure 19.3 Adult-led play

Assessment task 1.2

On the information poster about play, write down the difference between adult-led and child-centred play.

LO2 Factors that promote inclusive and stimulating play environments

2.1 Inclusive and stimulating play

To provide inclusive and stimulating play in a setting, care workers should understand the needs, interests, likes and dislikes of all children and young people in the group.

Inclusive play is when all children and young people in the group can enjoy taking part in the activity. Adults plan activities around the children's interests and make sure they meet their individual needs.

Stimulating play is when all children want to take part because the play activity looks interesting and fun to take part in.

Important words

Inclusive play – play activities that all children and young people can join in with

Stimulating play – play that is interesting and enjoyable

Task

In pairs, think about how cardboard boxes can be used to provide inclusive and stimulating play for children.

2.2 Environments that support inclusive and stimulating play

Both indoor and outdoor settings can support inclusive and stimulating play. It is important that there is a mixture of child-centred and adult-led play, so that children can enjoy activities that are planned by the adult and activities they choose for themselves.

A wide range of activities should be available for children and young people, so that they are given a choice of things that they enjoy and are able to do. It is also very important to have activities that the children and young people have not tried before so that they are able to have new experiences and develop new skills.

Care workers or nursery workers must think about the individual needs of children when they set out activities, toys and equipment so that all children can take part.

◆ Some children need to have special equipment to allow them to take part in an activity; for example, a child who is left-handed will need to have left-handed scissors when they are doing a cutting and sticking activity.

◆ If there is a young person who uses a wheelchair or who has a sight impairment, the furniture will need to be set out in a way that makes it easier for them to take part in the activity and move around safely.

Figure 19.4 Some children need to have special equipment to allow them to take part in an activity

Care workers are also an important part of the child's environment, so they should offer encouragement, praise the children and young people, and give them the right amount of help when they ask for it.

Assessment task 2.1 2.2

On the information poster about play, write down:
◆ the meaning of 'inclusive and stimulating play'
◆ what makes an environment 'inclusive and stimulating'.

2.3 Activities that promote inclusive and stimulating play

There are many types of play activities that allow all children to have fun and learn new skills.

These can include:

◆ *Creative play.* This is where children and young people use things such as crayons, paint, paper, glue or other materials to be creative. It also includes activities such as playdough, sand play, junk modelling, and cutting and sticking. It is important to remember that left-handed scissors should be available for children who are left-handed.

◆ *Physical play.* This is where children and young people can enjoy using their physical skills, such as running, jumping, catching and throwing. Physical play can be enjoyed in groups – for example, tag or hide and seek – and team games such as football or netball can help children to understand team work and develop their physical skills.

◆ *Imaginative play.* This is where children and young people pretend to be someone or somewhere else. Children and young people do not always need to have any equipment to enjoy imaginative play; for example, young children who are pretending that they are lions or tigers will just get down on the floor and make roaring noises.

Equipment and props, such as a home corner in a setting or an outside den, can help children to use their imagination. A young child may pretend that the cardboard box they are sitting in is a car, or a group of children may dress up as pirates and pretend the box is a boat on the high seas.

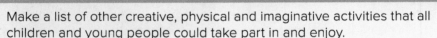

Assessment task 2.3

Make a list of other creative, physical and imaginative activities that all children and young people could take part in and enjoy.

Summary

In this unit, you have learned that:

◆ play supports children's and young people's development and well-being

◆ there is a difference between adult-led play and child-centred play

◆ environments can support inclusive and stimulating play

◆ activities support inclusive and stimulating play.

Chapter 20

CFC 19 Self development

LO1 How to recognise the significance of achievements and interests in relation to your own development

1.1 How to describe achievements and interests

Achievements

Our **achievements** are the things that we have successfully managed to do. For example, you may learn to swim or become good at gymnastics. Sometimes learning a new skill or understanding more about something may result in you achieving an award or getting a certificate.

Other achievements may be as simple as becoming more confident in different situations; for example, deciding to start a new college course or becoming more organised when preparing for an exam.

Important word

Achievement – something that you successfully managed to do

Task

In pairs, make a list of all your achievements in your life so far. Think about when you may have been afraid or anxious about trying something that you then successfully managed to do. Remember to include any qualifications, certificates or awards you have achieved.

Interests

Our interests help us to make choices about college courses or future work goals. You may enjoy spending time with older adults, and this could make you think that a job working in care of older adults would suit you.

When someone has an interest, they might do some research to find out more about it. For example, if you enjoy keeping fit, you might contact the local sports centre to find out about fitness classes or gym membership.

1.2 How your achievements and interests have supported your development

Case study

Salina is 15 years old and lives with her dad, her three sisters and her grandmother. Ever since she was very young, Salina has enjoyed helping her grandmother in the kitchen at home. Salina feels confident in helping to cook the family meals. This interest in cooking made Salina research cookery and catering courses that were available at her local college. Salina applied for a place on a cookery course, had a successful interview with the tutor and was offered a place on the course. Salina is looking forward to starting college in September.

Copy and complete Table 20.1 to show your achievements and interests, and to describe how these have supported your own development.

Achievement/interest	Ways that this has supported my development
Example: *Learning to touch type on a computer*	*This has helped me to confidently use a computer to complete school and college coursework. I can present my work in a professional way and easily make any changes.*

Table 20.1 How my achievements and interests have supported my development

LO2 How to recognise your own strengths and areas for further development

2.1 Your strengths in skills, qualities and abilities and their importance for the future

Skills

When caring for others, it is important to work professionally. This means having a wide range of **skills**, such as good communication, arriving at work on time, being clean and well-presented, and following **policies and procedures** correctly.

Qualities

It is also very important to have the right **qualities** for your chosen job role. For example, when working with babies and children, it is important to be a good role model because young children will often copy the people around them. When caring for older aged adults, it is important to listen to their views and opinions, and to show kindness and respect. Other key qualities are being patient and caring towards others around you.

Abilities

It is also important to have the right **abilities** for your role. When caring for others, it is essential that you are able to work well as part of a team. This means sharing ideas, supporting others in the team and making sure that all your work is done well.

Important words

Strengths – things we are good at

Areas for further development – things that we need to improve or get better at

Skills – something we are able to do well

Policies and procedures – the rules of the setting, which need to be followed at all times when caring for others

Qualities – good parts of our personality

Abilities – things we are able to do

2.2 Areas for development, and why and how they need to be improved

Sometimes you know that you do not have all the skills and knowledge that you need to be able to work in your chosen job role. When you become aware of this, you can decide on the best way to **make improvements**. For example:

◆ Ask your teacher if you do not understand something you are learning about.
◆ If you need to improve a skill, make time to practise it.
◆ If you know that your timekeeping or communication skills are not always good, think about what you can do to improve.

Important words

Make improvements – to get better at something

Case study

Jenna's personal goal is to work as a football coach for young children. She is occasionally late for college or forgets her ID badge, which must be worn. Jenna understands that arriving on time and being organised are skills that she must have if she wants to become a football coach. She thinks about how to improve on these areas of her development; she decides she must pack her college bag the night before to make sure she has everything she needs, including her badge, and must set her alarm an hour before she needs to leave the house.

Jenna's areas for improvement	Why they are important as a football coach	How improvements can be made by Jenna
Timekeeping	Football matches always have a certain start time	Setting the alarm on her phone as a reminder
Remembering to take her ID badge	It is important to have all the correct kit when playing sports	Packing her bag and organising her college things the night before

Table 20.2 Jenna's personal development plan

2.3 Match your skills, qualities and abilities to your chosen role

When thinking about a career in health care or childcare, it is important to think about your skills, qualities and abilities. Everyone working with children should be a good role model. Children copy the behaviours of others around them, so you must always follow the rules and be respectful to others.

◆ You must show children how to be kind and caring, by being kind and caring towards them.
◆ You must support children to manage their own behaviour by being patient and staying calm when children get angry or upset.

Everyone working in health care should think about the qualities and abilities they need to provide a high standard of care to service users. These include:

◆ being cheerful and happy around the individuals you are caring for
◆ being respectful and taking time to listen to a person's views and opinions
◆ working well as part of a team
◆ following all policies and procedures
◆ keeping records up to date and completing reports accurately when needed.

Sometimes when deciding to work in health care or childcare, we need to understand what we may need to change about ourselves. For example:

◆ If you sometimes use bad language or react to others in an aggressive way, you will need to work on changing these behaviours if you want a career with children, as these behaviours are not acceptable.
◆ If you have difficulty following rules – such as arriving at college on time and working well in lessons – you will need to change these behaviours before you are suitable to work in health and social care or childcare.

Task

In small groups, talk about and write down other skills, qualities and abilities you think you may need when choosing to work with babies and children.

Explain why each of these are important for:
◆ successfully completing a childcare course
◆ working well with babies and children.

Assessment task 2.1 2.2 2.3

1 List your own skills, qualities and abilities. Describe how they will help you to successfully complete courses and succeed in your chosen job role.
2 List your own areas for development (things you feel you are not doing well enough yet for the job role you have chosen) and describe ways to improve on these areas.

LO3 How your own learning style influences career and education choices

3.1 Your own learning style and how it influences your choices

Your own **learning style** is how you best learn something new; you may have more than one learning style that you use.

> ### Important words
>
> **Learning style** – the way we learn best; we may have more than one learning style

> ### Case study
>
> Courtney works with young children in a nursery and her supervisor has asked her to make some playdough with the children. This is something that Courtney has not done before. If Courtney is a **visual learner**, she may go online to see how dough is made and copy this. If she is an **auditory learner**, Courtney may ask her supervisor how to make it and listen to what she tells her. If Courtney learns best by **reading and writing**, she may look in a book for instructions and then write a plan. If Courtney is a **kinaesthetic learner**, she may use the ingredients to have a go before doing the activity with the children.

> ### Important words
>
> **Visual learner** – you learn best by looking at diagrams and symbols
>
> **Auditory learner** – you learn best by listening to information or taking part in group discussions, for example
>
> **Reading and writing learning style** – you learn best by reading information and taking notes
>
> **Kinaesthetic learner** – you learn best by having a go at something to try to understand it or watching someone else doing it

> ### Task
>
> Think about how you would best learn how to make playdough for the first time. This will help you to understand what your learning style(s) may be.

Copy and complete Table 20.3 below. You need to identify your own learning style(s) and describe ways that you can use this information to successfully complete your college course.

Task	Learning style(s)	Good ways to complete the task
Finding information to make a poster about child development		
Revising for a test		
Preparing to give a presentation to the rest of your group		
Planning a craft activity for adults with a learning disability		
Finding information to help you decide what you want to do after your college course		

Table 20.3 Identifying your learning styles and ways to successfully complete tasks

LO4 Set personal goals and objectives

4.1 4.2 Identify personal goals and describe their relevance

There are many ways to identify and set your own **personal goals** – for example, looking at the different job roles in your chosen career and finding out about the qualifications and skills you will need to do the job well.

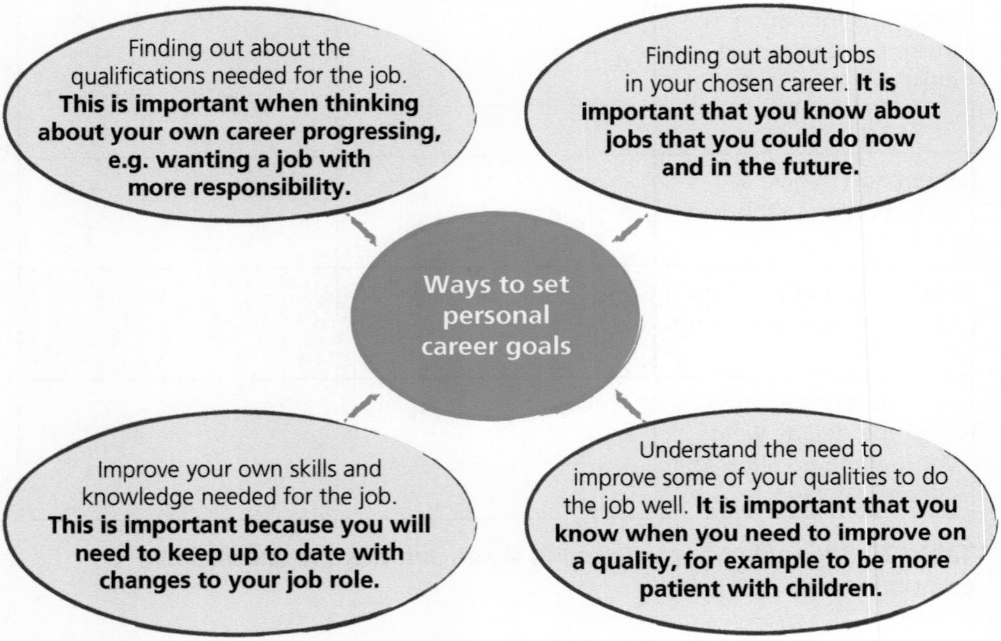
Finding out about the qualifications needed for the job. This is important when thinking about your own career progressing, e.g. wanting a job with more responsibility.
Finding out about jobs in your chosen career. It is important that you know about jobs that you could do now and in the future.
Ways to set personal career goals
Improve your own skills and knowledge needed for the job. This is important because you will need to keep up to date with changes to your job role.
Understand the need to improve some of your qualities to do the job well. It is important that you know when you need to improve on a quality, for example to be more patient with children.

Figure 20.1 Ways to set personal career goals

Important words

Personal goals – targets we want to achieve, such as getting a job or passing an exam

Assessment task 4.1 4.2

Draw a spider diagram like the one in Figure 20.1 to identify three personal goals. Describe why each goal is important for your own development in your chosen career.

5.1 Produce an action plan with SMART goals and actions to be taken

When you have identified your personal goals, you then need to think about how you can best achieve these goals. For example, once you have found out about the qualifications needed to do a job role, you might then start researching local college courses.

It is important to make a written **action plan** to list your goals. Goals need to be SMART so that you identify what your goal is and understand how and when you will achieve it.

> ## Important words
>
> **Action plan** – a plan we can make and use to help us reach our goals

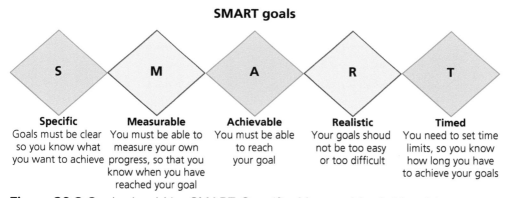

SMART goals

Specific	**Measurable**	**Achievable**	**Realistic**	**Timed**
Goals must be clear so you know what you want to achieve	You must be able to measure your own progress, so that you know when you have reached your goal	You must be able to reach your goal	Your goals shoud not be too easy or too difficult	You need to set time limits, so you know how long you have to achieve your goals

Figure 20.2 Goals should be SMART: Specific, Measurable, Achievable, Realistic and Timed

My goal is to learn to drive a car so that I can drive myself to work.	
Specific	I need to learn to drive to a safe standard.
Measurable	To pass the theory test and road test.
Achievable	I am 17 years old and I can afford to pay for the driving lessons.
Realistic	I have downloaded the theory app, I have time to learn and I have booked enough driving lessons.
Timed	I aim to pass my theory test within 6 months, and I hope to pass my driving test before I am 18 years old (in 11 months' time).

Table 20.4 An example of a SMART action plan

Action planning takes time; this can be a short or long time depending on your goal. When you have a long-term goal, such as learning to drive a car, it is important that you understand how long this might take. For example, you can have:

- a long-term goal (ten months) to pass your test
- a short-term goal (two weeks) to find an app to practise your driving theory knowledge.
- a medium-term goal (two months) to find a driving instructor and book a course of driving lessons.

Assessment task 5.1

Produce an action plan which identifies and records your personal goals which are SMART. Use Table 20.4 to help you.

Summary

In this unit, you have learned that:

- we use information about ourselves to choose our education and job role
- all our personal achievements and interests support our own development
- we all have things in our lives that we are good at – these are our strengths
- we all have areas to improve on and we can use SMART goals to do this
- we all have different skills, qualities and abilities, and knowing what these are can help us to choose a career
- there are four main learning styles: visual, auditory, read and write, and kinaesthetic
- writing a SMART action plan can help you to reach your goals.

Chapter 21

UNIT 11 Job opportunities in health and social care

What you will learn in this unit

You will gain an understanding of:
- the different job roles in health and social care
- the qualifications and skills needed for different job roles in health and social care
- starting work in health and social care.

LO1 LO2 LO3 Job opportunities, terms and conditions of employment, and the qualifications and skills needed within health and social care

1.1 The different jobs in health and social care

In health and social care, early years and childcare, there are many different job opportunities.
- To do some jobs, you will need to have lots of qualifications and experience. For example, to become a doctor who treats sick people or a physiotherapist who helps people recover from injury, you will need to study for many years at university.
- To do other jobs in the **care sector**, you may only need to have qualities such as patience and kindness, and not need qualifications to start the job. For example, a kind and caring person may be offered a job as a care home assistant and be sent on a training course to get a qualification while they are doing their job.

1.2 2.1 3.1 Examples of job roles and skills needed to do the job

Each job role in the care sector will require different qualifications, skills and experience. When working in the care sector, each job role will have a job description (sometimes called **terms and conditions**), which shows what the job role requires and the responsibilities of the person doing the job.

Health care sector

Residential care home manager – this role includes managing a team of care workers looking after older aged adults in a care home.

The skills needed for this job include being able to lead and support a team of care workers so they can offer a high standard of care to the older aged adults. Other skills include being able to manage the finances to make sure that money is spent well and the older aged adults have everything they need.

To apply for this job role, you need to have five years' experience working in a care home and have a care and management qualification. The job requires shift work and some overnight stays.

Social care sector

Social worker – this role includes working as part of a team to safeguard children in the local area.

The skills for this job include good communication and accurate report writing, to make sure all information about a child at risk is shared in a confidential way with other professionals.

To apply for this job role, you will need to have a social work qualification and a full UK driving licence. You may need to work some evenings and weekends.

Childcare sector

Lunchtime play leader – this role includes supervising children aged 7–11 years during the lunchtime break.

The skills for this job include being patient and caring, and being able to communicate with children effectively. Other skills include managing children's behaviour and staying calm when dealing with challenging behaviour or accidents and injuries.

To apply for this job role, you need to have experience of being around children, and be willing to get a first aid qualification and attend safeguarding training.

Choose one job role from each care sector. Find out about the skills and qualifications you need to do the job.

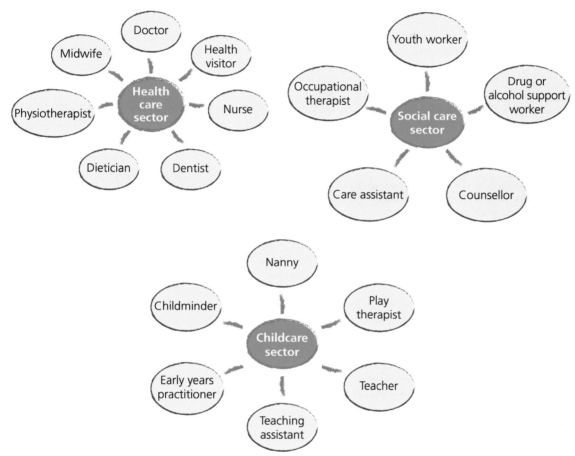

Figure 21.1 Different job roles in the care sectors

Task

Choose one job role from each care sector. Find out about the skills and qualifications you need to do the job.

LO4 How to start work within health and social care

4.1 Starting work in health and social care

Assessment task 4.1

Choose one care sector job role you would like to do in the future. Research the qualifications needed to do the job, and find out about the skills and experience you would also need.

In Table 21.1, identify a job role you would like to do. Write down the skills, qualities and training needed for the job and what you would need to do to be ready for this role. To help you, use the teacher role example given in the table.

Job role	Qualifications, skills and qualities needed for the job	My qualifications, skills and qualities	What I need to do to be ready for the job role
Teacher	◆ Teaching qualification ◆ Safeguarding training ◆ Good communication ◆ Organisational skills ◆ Ability to manage children's behaviour ◆ An understanding of the national curriculum, what children need to learn and how to assess learning	◆ Good communication ◆ I am reliable and organised ◆ I have done a safeguarding unit at college so understand something about child protection	◆ Do well at college so I can go to university to do a teaching qualification ◆ I need to learn about the national curriculum ◆ I need more experience in managing children's behaviour

Table 21.1 Qualifications, skills and qualities needed for the job

Summary

In this unit, you have learned that:

◆ there are many different job roles in health and social care

◆ there are certain qualifications and skills needed for different job roles in health and social care

◆ you need to understand the qualifications, skills and qualities needed to do your chosen job in the care sector.

Chapter 22

SHC 24 Introduction to duty of care in health, social care or children's and young people's settings

What you will learn in this unit

You will gain an understanding of:
- what is meant by 'duty of care'
- how the duty of care affects the way practitioners work
- dilemmas between duty of care and a person's rights, and how to solve these dilemmas
- how to handle complaints.

LO1 The implications of duty of care

1.1 1.2 The meaning of 'duty of care' and how it affects the way practitioners work

'Duty of care' means that there must be a high standard of care given to service users within the care sector. Practitioners must always work to the best of their ability to make sure the quality of their care is high. If there any reasons why a practitioner cannot offer high-quality care, they must report this to their manager.

The manager may decide the practitioner needs to go on a training course or watch the way other practitioners work to learn how to do the job to the best of their ability. This will make sure 'duty of care' is being carried out properly.

Example!

Jessie works in a day care centre supporting young people with learning difficulties. Jessie feels that she sometimes does not deal with challenging behaviour in a way that keeps the young people calm. She knows she has a 'duty of care' to provide the best support she can to the young people. Jessie tells her manager that she does not always feel confident when dealing with young people who are angry. Jessie's manager suggests she watches Nick, another care worker, who is very good at calming young people down when they are showing anger.

Assessment task 1.1 1.2

Produce a poster for a day care centre explaining:
◆ what 'duty of care' means
◆ what practitioners in the day care centre must do if they feel they could do their job better.

Figure 22.1 Training may be needed when a health care professional realises they need to know more about part of their job role

LO2 Support available for addressing dilemmas that may arise about duty of care

2.1 2.2 Dilemmas that may arise between the duty of care and a person's rights and how to resolve dilemmas

When there are problems in providing high-quality care, it is important for practitioners to quickly solve the problems and make sure 'duty of care' is of a high standard.

A **dilemma** could be when a person using a care service chooses to do something that will not be good for them or could cause them harm. Although the person has the right to choose what they do, the practitioner also has a duty of care to keep the person safe.

> ### Example!
>
> Bill, an adult with learning difficulties who also has diabetes, chooses to eat sweet, sugary foods, which he knows can make him very unwell.
>
> In this dilemma, the practitioner should try to make sure that Bill's food choices do not include sugar. This is not what Bill wants but the practitioner is showing a 'duty of care' in protecting Bill's health.
>
>

Getting additional support and advice

Sometimes, when practitioners have to deal with dilemmas, they may need to get advice from other professionals, such as doctors, dieticians and social workers. They may also get information from other sources, such as information centres, telephone helplines and recognised websites.

> ### Important word
>
> **Dilemma** – a problem

Julie, aged 19 years, has Down's syndrome. She lives in a house with three other young people who receive extra support from care workers. Over the last few months, Julie has been talking online to a new friend called Jo. Julie has asked her care workers if she can take a five-mile bus ride to meet up with Jo.

The care workers know it is important for Julie to make friends and be independent so would like Julie to be able to meet her friend. However, Julie has not been on a bus on her own before so her care workers are worried about her safety.

In pairs, make a plan for Julie that will allow her carers to keep her safe when she goes to meet Jo. In your plan, include information about where the carers could go for additional support and advice to **resolve the dilemma**.

Important words

Resolve the dilemma – a way to solve a problem

3.1 3.2 How to handle complaints

When working with children, young people and adults, there will always be times when **complaints** are made by service users. It is important that practitioners take complaints seriously because often by dealing with them, the service can improve. Complaints can be made in writing or by somebody saying they are unhappy with a service.

When a complaint is made, it is important to deal with it professionally. Every care service has **procedures** to follow when a complaint is made. When discussing a complaint, practitioners need to follow confidentiality procedures – this means not discussing the complaint with anyone other than their manager. Usually, it is only the manager who will deal with a complaint.

When working in the care service, it is important to find out about the setting's complaint policies and procedures, so you can deal with complaints in the right way.

Important words

Complaints – when someone reports that they are not happy with a service or the way another person does their job

Procedures – steps to take when doing a task

Steps to take when dealing with a complaint

1 Understand the complaint by listening carefully to the service user who is unhappy or by taking time to read the letter of complaint properly.
2 Let the person who is unhappy know that you take their complaint seriously and will pass this on to the manager straight away.
3 Do not discuss the complaint with others because practitioners must follow the setting's confidentiality policy.

Figure 22.2 It is important to listen carefully to a complaint

When the manager has dealt with the complaint, they will usually meet the person who was unhappy to let them know what is being done about the complaint. Sometimes, the way care is given in the setting may be changed to make sure the same complaint is not made in the future.

Figure 22.3 Children in a day nursery

Assessment task 3.1 3.2

You are working in a children's day nursery. The manager has asked you to make a poster for the parent's noticeboard about the complaints procedure. In the poster, include:

◆ what the parents should do if they are unhappy with any of the care provided by the nursery staff

◆ how the staff will deal with any complaints made by parents.

Summary

In this unit, you have learned that:

◆ 'duty of care' means that care provided must be of a high standard

◆ practitioners working in the care service must always work to the best of their ability to provide high-quality care

◆ there will always be times when practitioners have dilemmas between giving the best standard of care and the personal choices individuals sometimes make

◆ it is important to deal with complaints professionally by always following the setting's complaints policies and procedures.

Glossary

Abilities – things we are able to do

Abuse – to be treated in a damaging way by one or more people

Achievement – something that you successfully managed to do

Action plan – a plan we can make and use to help us reach our goals

Adult-led play – play activities that are planned and run by adults

Antioxidant – this works to reverse the damage that pollution has on the body

Areas for further development – things that we need to improve or get better at

Assessing risk – seeing something that might be a danger to someone

Assist – help

Auditory learner – you learn best by listening to information or taking part in group discussions, for example

Balanced diet – daily food that has the right amount of nutrients for health and growth

Barrier – something that gets in a person's way and may stop them from doing something

Behavioural characteristics – the types of behaviour a person shows

Care sector – health care, social care and childcare are all different care sectors that people may work in

Challenging discriminatory attitudes – telling people who treat individuals with disability in an unkind way that they are wrong and must change their attitude or behaviour

Child-centred play – play that is started and led by children themselves

Child-centred practice – meeting children's individual needs and understanding their interests so they can enjoy taking part in activities

Communication methods – ways to communicate

Complaints – when someone reports that they are not happy with a service or the way another person does their job

Confidentiality – only sharing information with people who need to know or can offer help

Contribute – help to support

COSHH – the law linking to the **C**ontrol **o**f **S**ubstances that are **H**azardous to **H**ealth

Dehydrated – dried out and thirsty

Dementia – a disease that damages the brain, causing a person to forget things, be unable to think clearly or lose the ability to speak

Department of Health – a government department that is concerned with the health of the UK's citizens

Dependent – needing the help and support of others

Dietician – a person who gives advice on healthy food and diet

Dilemma – a problem

Discriminatory attitude – when someone judges another person or group of people because of the way they look, how they speak, their age, the clothes they choose to wear or who they choose to have a relationship with, for example

Discriminatory behaviour – when someone treats another person or group of people differently because of the way they look, how they speak, the music they listen to or the clothes they choose to wear, for example

Effective communication – giving information in a way that best suits an individual

Emotional and social well-being – happiness in yourself and as part of a group (society)

Employee – a worker

Employer – someone or an organisation that pays workers for their work

Employment – a job that you are paid to do

Environment – the space around the child

Equality – making sure all people are treated fairly

Evacuate – leave a building or area safely

Expected pattern of development – the order in which most people develop

Factors – negative or positive things that may have happened

First aider – someone with a first aid qualification

Formal communication – when information is shared in a professional way; slang words are not used

Guidance and standards – rules and guidelines that should be followed

Harm – injury or hurt caused to someone

Hinder – stop

Inclusion – being part of something, and making sure everyone is included in a fair and equal way

Inclusive play – play activities that all children and young children can join in with

Independent – not always needing the help and support of others

Informal communication – speaking with friends

Informing individuals – letting people know

Interests and preferences – the things that a person enjoys and chooses to do

Job role – the job that somebody working in the care sector does

Kinaesthetic learner – you learn best by having a go at something to try to understand it or watching someone else doing it

Learning style – the way we learn best; we may have more than one learning style

Legislation – laws or rules which must be followed

Leisure activities – interests or hobbies that people can enjoy

Life event – something that has happened to a person that has affected their life, such as serious illness or loss of a family member

Lifestyle – way of life

Make improvements – to get better at something

Mental Capacity Act – a law made to protect people who are experiencing poor mental health

Mental health – how a person's thinking makes them feel

Neglect – when someone is not looked after or cared for properly

Non-verbal communication – ways to communicate without speaking

Nutrients – found in food; they do an important job to keep the body healthy

Nutritional allergies – when a baby or child becomes ill from eating or touching a certain food

Nutritional needs – the food a baby or child needs to grow and stay healthy

Partnership working – when different professionals with different knowledge and skills work together to best support service users

Pathway – a timeline

Personal goals – targets we want to achieve, such as getting a job or passing an exam

Person-centred approach – understanding a person's individual needs and caring for them in the way that suits them best

Person-centred practice – listening to a person and meeting their individual needs in the way that is best for them

Physical barrier – when someone is stopped from taking part in an activity because the environment and/or equipment does not meet their individual needs

Physical care routines – a baby's or child's day-to-day care needs (skin, hair, teeth, nappy area)

Policies and procedures – the rules of the setting, which need to be followed at all times when working with babies and children

Preventing – trying to stop something from happening

Principles and values – the main beliefs and ideas of an organisation

Procedures – steps to take when doing a task

Progression (in a career) – being able to move on to the job you want to do, or to get a promotion

Promoting independence – encouraging someone to find ways to do things for themselves

Qualifications and skills – the training or courses you need to complete and the things you need to be good at to do the job well

Qualities – good parts of our personality

Reading and writing learning style – you learn best by reading information and taking notes

Recommended daily fluid intake – the amount of water that experts say we should drink every day

Releases – frees

Research – finding information, for example, from the internet, from books or by speaking to others

Resilience – being able to cope with a situation or feeling

Resolve the dilemma – a way to solve a problem

Respecting and valuing – to show care and consideration of others' views and opinions

Routines – tasks or activities which happen regularly during the day, usually at a set time; for example, mealtimes and bedtimes

Safe and hygienic environment – keeping the space around the baby or child clean and making sure they are safe from harm

Safe disposal – to throw away safely

Safeguarding – protecting children and adults from harm, abuse or neglect

Safety control – things that can be done to reduce the risk of injury

Self-esteem – feeling good about yourself and having confidence

Sensory difficulties – difficulties individuals have when using one or more of the five senses (touch, smell, taste, sight, hearing)

Service provision – services that are available for people needing health care, social care or childcare

Service user – someone who uses the health, social or childcare services

Skills – something we are able to do well

Social activities – activities that people take part in with others

Social barrier – the way people are treated by others which can stop them being included or taking part in an activity

Stamina – the strength and energy people need to do physical activity

Stimulating play – play that is interesting and enjoyable

Strengths – things we are good at

Supervise – to watch a baby or child to make sure they are staying safe

Support organisations – organisations such as Childline, the NSPCC and Women's Aid which work to protect children and adults

Support relationships – spending time with others to strengthen friendships and meet new people

Team work – when people work well together

Terms and conditions – this lists what you are expected to do in a certain job role and will be written down in a job description

Verbal communication – speaking and listening

Visual communication systems – form of communication that includes the use of pictures to support communication and understanding

Visual learner – you learn best by looking at diagrams and symbols

Vulnerable adult – someone who could be abused easily or hurt through neglect or unkindness

Well-being – an individual's good physical and mental health

Index

development
  emotional 100, 105–9, 114, 118
  factors affecting 101–3, 110–14
  intellectual 99–100, 105–9,
    114, 117
  language 105–9, 110, 114, 116
  life stages 97–9
  patterns of 104–9
  physical 99, 105–9, 114–15
  and play 185
  social 100, 105–9, 114, 118
  supporting 114–18
diet 87–91, 101, 111, 128–9, 182
dietician 82
dilemmas, duty of care 207–8
disability 56, 113
  see also physical disability
discrimination
  attitudes 50–2, 149
  behaviours 53–4
doctor
  job role 10, 82
  see also GP (general practitioner)
Down's syndrome 208
duty of care 205–10
  complaints 209–10
  dilemmas 207–8

E

Early Years Foundation Stage
  (EYFS) 16, 49
eating disorders 155
Eatwell Guide 182
emergency services 2
emotional abuse 26, 28
emotional development 100,
  105–9, 114, 118
employees, responsibilities 59
employers, responsibilities 58
employment
  and development 114
  job roles 9–13
  progression routes 12–13
environment
  and development 113
  and physical disability 148
  and play 188–9
environmental barriers 46
equality 48–9, 145–6, 153

barriers to 56–7
  promoting 57
Equality Act 2010 16, 49, 145,
  153
evacuation 59
exclusion 53
  see also inclusion
exercise 101, 112, 129

F

family relationships 111
fats 88–9
fire safety 59
first aid 60–1
fluid intake 92–5
food groups 87–9, 181–2
foot allergies 183
formal communication 41
foster care 2
fronto-temporal dementia 162
  see also dementia
fruit 88–9, 181–2
fussy eaters 182

G

General Data Protection
  Regulation (GDPR) 21, 49
genetic disability 144
goals 198–200
GP (general practitioner) 3, 33, 82
grief 162–3
group discussions 39, 42
guidance and standards 15–17

H

hair care 171–2
hand-washing 64, 71
harm 26
hazardous substances 62
hazards 66–7
head lice 172
health, and development 111
health and safety
  accidents and illness 69–70
  fire safety 59
  first aid 60–1
  hazardous substances 62

hazards 66–7
  infection prevention 64, 71
  medication 63
  moving and handling 60, 68–9
  personal protective equipment
    (PPE) 72
  risk assessment 62, 66–7, 78
  risks 66
  safety controls 78
  security 61, 68
  training 65
  waste disposal 64
Health and Social Care Act 2012
  17, 49
health care assistant 10
health care job roles 10, 202–3
health centre 82
healthy eating 87–91, 128–9
  see also diet
history, of service user 75
hobbies 120–7
hospitals, accident and emergency
  department 2
housing 113
human growth 97–9

I

illness 69–70, 101, 112, 144
imaginative play 190
inclusion 48–9, 56–7, 152–3
inclusive play 188
independence 78–9, 104, 127,
  151–2, 175
  see also person-centred
    practice
independent services 7
infancy 97
infection prevention 64, 71
informal care 7–8
informal communication 40
information
  sharing 21, 30–1
  see also confidentiality
intellectual development 99–100,
  105–9, 114, 117
interests 192
  of service user 124